WATER WARS

The Fight to Control and Conserve
Nature's Most Precious Resource

OLGA COSSI

AN EARTHCARE BOOK

New Discovery Books
New York

Maxwell Macmillan Canada
Toronto

Maxwell Macmillan International
New York   Oxford   Singapore   Sydney

Cover photo: Rick Mastelli
Cover and book design: Deborah Fillion
Copyright © 1993 by Olga Cossi

New Discovery Books
Macmillan Publishing Company
866 Third Avenue
New York, NY 10022

Maxwell Macmillan Canada, Inc.
1200 Eglinton Avenue East
Suite 200
Don Mills, Ontario M3C 3N1

Macmillan Publishing Company is part of
the Maxwell Communication Group of Companies.

First edition
Printed in the United States of America
10 9 8 7 6 5 4 3 2 1

Library of Congress Cataloging-in-Publication Data
Cossi, Olga.
    Water wars : the fight to control and conserve nature's most precious resource / by Olga Cossi. — 1st ed.
        p.   cm.
    Includes bibliographical references and index.
    Summary: Discusses water's sources, uses, and shortages; water quality problems and management programs; and what individuals can do to ensure cleaner water.
    ISBN 0-02-724595-0
    1. Water-supply—Juvenile literature.   2. Water quality—Juvenile literature.   3. Water conservation—Juvenile literature. [1. Water.   2. Water supply.   3. Water quality management.   4. Water conservation. 5. Conservation of natural resources.]   I. Title.
TD348.C67 1993
333.91—dc20   92-43968

To all librarians,

and especially to the staff

at the Coronado Public Library

ACKNOWLEDGMENTS

The author wishes to thank the following people for their support in the creation of this book:

Liz Horney (project consultant), Selma Jacobson (research assistant), David Buckovetz (teen editor), Beverly Komarek (League of Women Voters), Dr. Melville Frishberg (project consultant), Monica Sullivan (League of Women Voters), Catherine Compton (Concern Inc.), Wayne B. Solley (U.S. Geological Survey), Susan Seacrest (National Groundwater Foundation), Mark Statler (San Diego Water Authority), Sandra Postel (Worldwatch Institute), Gary Hofer (Los Angeles Metropolitan Water District), Beth Stein (Friends of the Earth), Mitchell M. Kodama (Los Angeles Department of Water and Power), Stephen F. Mack (Santa Barbara Water Supply Development), Robert Delk (Bureau of Indian Affairs), Steve Tant (U.S. Department of the Interior), Bela G. Liptak (Federation to Protect the Hungarian Environment), David Merritt, Jr. (The Witchita *Eagle*), Randell F. Piazza (Wastewater Management System), Joyce R. Starr (Global

Water Summit Initiative), Rita Schmidt Sudman (*Western Water* magazine), Rusty Black (Parks and Recreational Department of Lubbock, Texas), Darwyn H. Briggs (U.S. Department of Agriculture, Drough Response), Doris Selden (Chula Vista Elementary School District), Marianne Anderson (Freshwater Foundation), Peter J. Piecuck (Water Pollution Control Federation), Tim Westman (Wastewater Management), David Precht (*Bassmaster* magazine), the *Christian Science Monitor*, Environmental Protection Agency, American Water Works, Water Education Foundation, National Research Council, The World Bank, International Desalination Association, American Water resources Association, The American Ground Water Trust, The Institute of Water Research, Soil and Water Conservation Society, and the Isaak Walton League.

CONTENTS

AUTHOR'S NOTE

Before jumping off the deep end into a deep subject like water, I had a great respect for this natural resource. Now, after months of research, I have an even greater respect. I am also more hopeful that fresh, clean water has a future. I found through my research that a great number of young people are learning to respect water as a very special resource. They are becoming more and more aware of the problems that endanger the environment and our natural resources. Through education, young people are preparing to do the cleanup job previous generations have laid on their shoulders, and to do so fairly, balancing economic costs against environmental costs. I would be pleased if this book became part of that educational process.

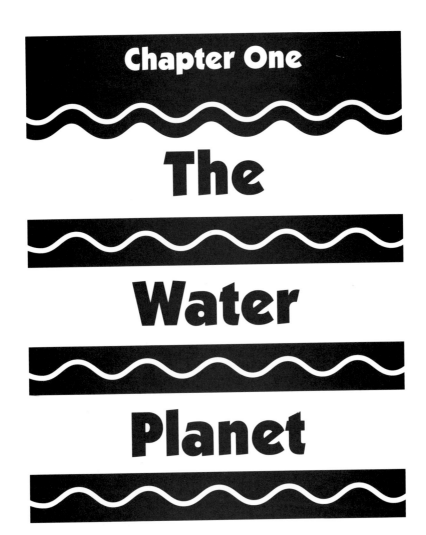

Chapter One

The Water Planet

A N EXPLOSION OCCURRED IN THE 1960S THAT WAS AS ENVIRON-
mentally significant as the dropping of the first atomic
bomb. The explosion took place in the American public's
attitude, creating a new social awakening that, among other
things, shattered the myth that natural resources are inexhaustible. Since that decade of realization, life on earth has
not been the same. Thirty years later we are still experiencing the fallout of that "big bang."

Water—fresh, clean water—has joined the list of endangered species. Finally, it is becoming appreciated as an indis-
pensable, finite resource, without which human life as we
know it could not exist.

Why is fresh, unpolluted water so important to everything and everyone?

To answer this question it is necessary to realize that of
all the planets known to man, earth alone deserves to be
called the water planet. It also helps to know something
about water itself and the role of fresh water as the cause
and source of life on earth.

Every living thing on this unique planet has a water con-
nection. Our bodies are 80 percent water. It lubricates our
systems, keeps them free from waste, and maintains a normal body temperature. Trees are 70 percent water and are
as reliant upon it as we are. Every living cell is water dependent, is water sustained, and therefore is vitally affected by
the quality and quantity of water available. Water, in fact,
instead of love, is what really makes the world go 'round.

Earth's wonderful **hydrological cycle** (the process in which water is used up and renewed) is both simple and complex. It can be described in one word—circulatory. Circulatory means recycling, a word that is increasingly becoming part of the general public's vocabulary. In nature, recycling is a built-in part of the system. It is the way water in changing forms and functions is used and reused over and over again as it maintains and sustains all living things. Water is such an indestructible substance that molecules created billions of years ago are still circulating today.

Scientists tell us that there are 326 million cubic miles of water in earth's hydrological cycle. Scientific studies have concluded that after earth's molten core cooled, water began to form and the rains came, falling for perhaps millions of years. Somehow enough hydrogen, which is the lightest of elements, was held in earth's gravity to combine with oxygen to form that miracle substance known as H_2O.

Water continues to be a miracle. The process by which it is formed is understood, but why that process happened, and why it happened only on this planet, is open to continued scientific thought and study. Everything had to be just right for earth to become the water planet, and apparently it was.

Ninety-seven percent of earth's water is salty and is contained largely in the oceans and seas that cover about 71 percent of earth's surface. Of the remaining fresh water, 2 percent is ice, held in a frozen state in glaciers, snow, and the ice cap of the Arctic. That leaves less than one percent available to meet the daily needs of plants, animals, and humans. Such a small percentage doesn't sound like enough, yet it amounts to about two million cubic miles of water, a staggering amount considering that each cubic mile

contains 1.1011 trillion gallons of life-sustaining wetness.

Circulation is a continual process that begins with pre-cipitation, better known as rainfall and snow, and completes its cycle in **evaporation**. Evaporation changes the liquid form of water into a gas that can then rise and become part of the moisture held and released by rain clouds. It is the warmth of the sun that causes water molecules to turn into steam or vapor. This change of form takes place constantly on the surface of all bodies of water, and on all wet surfaces of any kind, no matter how large or how small.

Clouds capture the rising vaporous moisture at a rate of 340 cubic miles a day. This is then released and recycled to earth in the form of rain, mist, fog, dew, frost, hail, and snow. The average length of time a water molecule is held in the air before it is released and recycled is roughly ten days. Each of these molecules has two atoms of hydrogen and one of oxygen. It is the "wetness" of the oxygen in the H_2O formula that sustains life.

Forests act as natural water reservoirs and are an impor-tant part of earth's hydrological system. The leaves and branches of trees catch a great amount of rainfall that would otherwise run off into streams. When the trees shed this moisture on the surface of the ground, branches soften the downpour and allow the earth to soak it up slowly. Some of the water is held in the thick layer of **duff** that forms the mulch covering forest floors. There it is protected from evaporation, allowing it to be used by the trees and under-growth as needed. The same moisture-holding action is true of jungles, woodlands, parks or planted areas, and of sur-faces covered with grass or other types of growth.

Trees and plants also absorb water through their root sys-tems. The moisture that is not used up by the trees or plants

themselves is returned to the atmosphere through **transpiration**, or sweating, that takes place on the surface of the leaves. Transpiration and evaporation combined are called *evapotranspiration,* which refers to the collective return into the hydrological cycle of vapor rising from the soil from bodies of surface water, plants, and trees. Of the 4.2 million gallons per day of rainfall recorded in the United States excluding Alaska and Hawaii, more than half is discharged into the atmosphere through evapotranspiration.

Rivers are the main waterways that sustain vast areas of land with life-giving moisture as they carry unused rainfall back to the oceans. They also recharge and/or are recharged by underground springs and serve as major factors in earth's ecology. During summer months in areas where there is little or no rain, the snow and ice packs that form in the mountains and higher elevations slowly melt and find their way into rivers, smaller streams, and lakes, helping to keep them alive and fresh. In less arid zones, seasonal monsoons and storms provide much of the annual water supply.

While rivers carry water back to the sea, they also carve canyons—some of them, like the Grand Canyon of Arizona, a mile deep. Rivers shape the land they flow through and determine if it will be rich and productive or dry and barren. Through floods they carry and deposit particles of soil, sand, silt, and clay, an estimated one million tons a day. Soil has been deposited in this manner since the beginning of time and affects the quality and availability of water resources.

Rainfall varies widely from region to region, from state to state, and from year to year. An overall average of about three feet of water falls each year per square foot of earth's surface. Of that, six inches finds its way to the seas and two feet evaporates and turns into water vapor. Rising molecules

75 percent of all the water used in a household flows through the bathroom. To help conserve water, install a low-flow shower head. This will save between 500 and 800 gallons a month. Cutting one minute from your shower time will save an additional 700 gallons a month.

of vapor are trapped in the atmosphere by cosmic dust and form clouds. The remaining six inches moistens the soil and recharges the underground reservoirs, called **aquifers**.

As rainwater or snowmelt soaks down through earth's surface, it follows the path of least resistance. It trickles and seeps through porous rock and deposits of sand and gravel, eventually gathering in an underground cavity or in the layers of sand and gravel that serve as aquifers.

About 90 percent of the world's supply of fresh water comes from such underground reservoirs. In the United States, we depend on groundwater for 95 percent of our

total fresh-water needs. For every gallon of surface water available, there are an estimated 24 gallons in underground reservoirs. Water held in such reservoirs can be **potable**, of drinking quality, or **nonpotable**, not fit for human consumption.

The surface depth at which groundwater can be reached is called the **water table** and is determined by drilling holes and measuring the level to which the water rises. A drop in the water table indicates that water is being withdrawn faster than it is recharged. In recent years, this has been happening in many parts of the United States and the world.

Sometimes an aquifer is confined, meaning that the water is more or less trapped between impermeable or water resistant layers of rock or clay formations. **Confined aquifers** are filled through a break or channel in the rock, always from a higher level and often from a considerable distance. Such confined bodies of subterranean water are under great pressure and are the source of **artesian** or free-flowing wells.

An **unconfined aquifer** is not surrounded by hard rock so it is recharged by water seeping into it from directly above, ordinarily from a saturated layer of permeable material or from surface water resources such as springs, streams, ponds, lakes, or rivers located anywhere at a higher elevation.

Groundwater moves slowly, usually only about three inches a day, seeping from less porous to more porous formations and layers of sand, gravel, or clay. Sometimes it is moved by **capillary action** that can cause a more rapid flow. An example of a capillary is a root that has grown through a crack in a rock and serves as a vessel to draw water. No matter how groundwater moves, the direction is

influenced by the force of gravity and is generally down-ward. Once water is trapped in a cavity inside the earth, it becomes an underground reservoir, where it remains until withdrawn or until it seeps into a stream or river and finds its way to the sea. When this happens, evaporation eventu-ally carries it upward again, where the moisture is captured in rain clouds to complete the hydrological cycle that makes earth such a unique water planet.

Chapter Two

Are We Running Out?

I F 71 PERCENT OF THE EARTH IS COVERED WITH WATER, WHY ARE so many areas of the United States and the world experiencing shortages and having to compete for fresh water?

One of the major reasons is that fresh-water resources are not evenly distributed. Some areas have large amounts, others very little. Within some national boundaries there can be rain forests and tropical jungles where everything grows lush and green, but there can also be vast deserts and arid regions with little rainfall and limited amounts of surface and groundwater.

In the United States, uneven distribution is found from state to state and within individual states where one part is arid and another has abundant water resources. This condition is not uncommon and means that water has to be imported from outside that area to fill water needs.

In California, 20 million residents depend on surface water supplies often transported hundreds of miles. Florida's coastal counties have water-quality problems because of salt-water intrusion in the public water supply, so water is piped many miles from inland resources. In such cases, there is often political conflict within the state as to who should get what share of available resources and if the proposed use is beneficial to the state as a whole.

Another major reason for shortages and competition is the growth of human populations. Earth's water resources do not increase. Human populations do. This increase in

recent years and its effect on water resources have caused widespread concern.

The world population figure reached the five billion mark in 1987 for the first time. It took centuries to get there, but by the year 2050 an additional five billion human inhabitants will have been added to earth's total. This means that each year the world increases by 90 million people, as much as the entire populace of Mexico.

The result of this population increase is that today almost every country is confronted with a growing demand for water. This is particularly true of those areas that are undeveloped. An undeveloped country is one that lacks technological advances and is dependent mainly on agriculture, the most water-intensive industry in the world. Africa, for instance, is expected to triple its percentage of the world population in spite of an extremely high infant death rate, which is linked to the quantity and quality of water available.

In Beijing, China, the water table is dropping at an alarming rate, and one-third of the city's wells have gone dry. Two hundred major cities in China have water shortages. India's fourth largest city, Madras, has only one public water tap, and its flow is restricted to the hours of 4 to 6 A.M. daily. Eight thousand villages in India have no local water at all, and people must walk to the nearest resource to supply their needs. And Egypt, where the present population of 35 million is increasing by another million every eight months, appears to be headed for a tragic water shortage crisis.

In spite of high technological advances and an abundant water supply, the United States has its share of problems trying to match its resources with the growing human demand. Problems are beginning to show up in almost every state, even though most water shortages are occurring west of the

Mississippi River, where population growth and arid conditions place pressure on the resources. Eight states, all but one located in the West, account for two-thirds of the total national groundwater withdrawal. Eight states, four in the West and four in the East, account for 41 percent of the total national surface water withdrawal.

Where is all the water going? What is it being used for?

The term **offstream usage** means that the water used is withdrawn or diverted from a main resource and piped or delivered to the point of need. Offstream water users can be broken down into four major categories that compete for fresh-water resources. These are agriculture, domestic and commercial needs, industry, mining, and **thermoelectrical power generation**.

In the United States, these four major categories of users combined add up to the withdrawal of more than 338,000 million gallons of fresh water a day from surface and groundwater resources. Only about 27 percent of the water withdrawn by them is consumptively, or actively, used. The remainder immediately becomes part of the return flow that is recycled. Water that is consumptively used is incorporated into products, crops, humans, or livestock and therefore is temporarily, but not permanently, removed from the hydrological cycle. There is virtually no permanent loss of water withdrawn for human use. It may change physical state, condition, and location several times, but eventually it will be released back into the environment.

Instream usage means that water is not withdrawn from a resource but used right in the channel itself. **Hydroelectrical power generation** is by far the major use in this category. The falling water that drives the turbines in a hydroelectric power facility immediately becomes part of

the return flow of its source, and none of it is consumptively used.

Hydroelectrical generation accounts for such a great volume of water, at least ten times that of any other instream users, that it dominates rather than competes with them. For this reason it is not included in this comparison.

The situation regarding instream use may change because of the recent increased emphasis on classifying a few of the other instream needs, such as for wildlife, fisheries, and the environment, as beneficial. The word "beneficial" is the key to this possible change. If that classification is officially recognized and becomes a federal law, then these needs will have a fair chance at least to compete with hydroelectrical plants for instream fresh-water use.

On a worldwide scale, agriculture accounts for the greatest percentage of total fresh water withdrawn. The global estimate is 41.8 percent, more than half of which is consumptively used. In the western United States, agriculture accounts for as much as 90 percent of withdrawal.

Agriculture uses most of its water for **irrigation**, the oldest technological practice known to the human race. Irrigation makes it possible for farmers to grow fibers such as cotton, linen, and wool to clothe people, and more importantly, the food to feed them. Without irrigation, food production would have no chance of keeping up with population growth and the national or global demand to satisfy hunger.

Food production and processing are water-intensive, meaning they require a great amount of water to get from the field to the table. For example, it may take only a few minutes to stop at a fast-food counter and order a hamburger, french fries, and a soft drink, but it takes 1,500 gal-

Toilets use a lot of water to flush. Putting a brick into the toilet tank will lower the amount needed to fill the tank, saving 8 to 20 gallons per person each day. Fixing a leaky toilet will save 200 gallons a month, and a dripping faucet up to 600 gallons a month.

lons of water to grow and process the products that make each single order possible.

Thermoelectrical power plants are second to agriculture in national water withdrawal, accounting for 38.7 percent, relatively little of which is consumptively used. Unlike hydroelectrical generation, thermoelectrical plants do not rely entirely on fresh water. In many cases they use saline water. Power is produced by steam using fossil fuel, nuclear, or geothermal energy. Most of the water used is for condenser and reactor cooling. The amount needed depends on whether the water is recycled through cooling towers or ponds and reused, or if it is used on a once-through system.

Domestic and commercial needs account for 10.4 per-

cent of the total national water withdrawal, a little over one-fifth of which is consumptively used. Since people tend to congregate in warm climates regardless of the availability of fresh-water resources, cities and congested suburbs in arid regions have to compete more intensely for an adequate and safe supply of water.

Household use heads the list of a city's domestic needs. The average American family living in the average American city uses an average of 170 gallons of water a day per person. The highest per person use in the world is in Beverly Hills, California, where each resident accounts for up to 500 gallons a day. By comparison, in Europe that figure is only 25 gallons. And in developing countries, where water is available, the daily average can be as low as five gallons.

The difference in usage is due to life-style. In the United States, indoor plumbing, flush toilets, showers, dishwashers, and garbage disposals are generally taken for granted. In many homes, swimming pools, hot tubs, and outdoor sprinkler systems are the norm. These modern conveniences use a lot of water, particularly flush toilets, which take from five to seven gallons per flush.

Commercial needs include public services such as medical facilities, schools, hotels, motels, office buildings, restaurants, and a variety of civilian and military institutions. California ranks first nationwide in both domestic and commercial use, as it does in almost all categories of water use.

Industry and mining account for 9.1 percent of the total national water withdrawal, a comparatively small part of which is consumptively used. Most industrial water is used for manufacturing steel and primary metals, chemicals, paper products, and for refining petroleum. Automobiles head the list of things the American public especially can't

do without. One hundred thousand gallons of water go into the production of each car before it is ready to roll off the assembly line and into a service station or someone's garage.

In mining, water is used to extract coal, oil, gas, metals, and inorganic minerals, and for the various steps in processing and manufacturing products. In some states, such as Tennessee, sand and gravel operations and clay mining are major water users. In South Dakota, gold production makes it a leader in the mining of that precious metal. The location of the natural deposits determines the location of the mines, whether it happens to be in a water-rich region or an arid region.

Water for mining is used in various ways and in various amounts depending on the methods of extraction and processing needed. Steel, for instance, is a water-intensive product. Mining the raw material and producing the finished steel for just one car takes 32,000 gallons of water. For one 30-pound bicycle, it takes 480 gallons.

Several lesser instream needs, those with less political or economic priority, have been losing out until very recently in the competition for fresh-water resources, among them recreation, wildlife, and ecology/environment. All of these needs are for instream use and very little of the water is consumptively used.

Swimming, waterskiing, and boating are three sports high on the list of reasons why recreation is in the competition for water. So are river rafting, kayaking, and canoeing. Fresh-water fishing is another popular recreational sport and is the favorite pastime of 65 million Americans. Familiar streams, rivers, and lakes are hallowed spots to which fishermen return year after year, whether it is to a catfish pond in Mississippi or a trout stream in Montana. Many of

these water resources are competing desperately for water to provide for the needs of many different species of freshwater fish.

One of the most intense competitions for water resources pits the Northwest salmon against many other users. Salmon species born hundreds of miles up the Columbia and Snake river system in Washington and Idaho have three weeks to make it downstream while their biological clocks are still running. Driven by instinct, they must get past 56 major dams on the 260,000-square-mile Columbia River watershed, almost every inch of the way also competing with agricultural interests, industry, and commercial navigation. Those that make it spend two or three years migrating to the Pacific Northwest and back. By then they are mature enough to try to return to their place of birth and spawn.

Neither fish ladders nor fish hatcheries make up for the salmon's need for increased flow of water at key times during their reproductive cycle. With so much against them, the annual Columbia River run has declined by 85 percent, and most of those remaining are hatchery fish known locally as "swimming hot dogs."

Other species of wildlife fighting for their water rights in the United States range from **migratory** birds—which depend on wetlands, swamps, and ponds to rest and feed on their long flights—to alligators in the Florida Everglades, which is fast running out of water.

Wildlife's competition for water is not limited to the United States. It is a growing international concern, as is seen in the case of the baiji, the Chinese river dolphin, the rarest of this species of animals. At one time baiji were common in other locations as well as the Yangtze River. Now the

If you leave the water running while you brush your teeth, you're wasting water. Turn the faucet off while you brush, and save 3 gallons a brush.

dolphins are found only in the Yangtze and their population is down to an estimated 300 adults and young.

The latest threat to the baiji comes from the proposed building of the Three Gorges dam on the Yangtze River. The project has been approved by the National People's Congress and is China's most controversial public development in modern times. If completed, it would be the world's largest dam. Critics warn that the cost will match its size, both financially and environmentally. But officials in China hail the project as a symbol of socialism's grand design for the masses, even though the people have no voice in the matter. It goes without saying that the Chinese river dolphins have no voice in the matter either.

Following a recent workshop on the baiji, biologists concluded that pollution, the reduction of fish population, the loss of water from drainage for farmland, and now the Three Gorges dam have made extinction almost inevitable. Obvi-

ously, wildlife's competition for fresh-water resources involves the same general factors regardless of where it is happening.

Scientists who monitor the environment warn that the earth cannot afford to lose out any longer in the competition for fresh water. Underground aquifers, wetlands, and rivers in particular require great amounts of fresh, clean water to survive as components of the hydrological cycle.

Aquifers need to be recharged regularly. The Ogallala, a vast reservoir that underlies 225,000 square miles of the Midwest from South Dakota to Texas and supplies enough water to turn that "Great American Desert" into an 800-mile greenbelt of farms, is in need of being replenished before the water table drops any lower. In some areas, such as the southwest corner of Kansas where the water table has declined about 200 feet in the past 45 years, there is critical concern by environmentalists and by those farmers who depend on the Ogallala for their water.

Wetlands are more than habitats for wildlife. They lessen the effects of floods and storms by absorbing excess water, they trap the movement of sediment and help prevent erosion, and they filter water before allowing it to seep into soil and recharge aquifers or streams. Wetlands need water to survive.

When the Clean Water Act was reauthorized in 1977, the first statutory mention of wetlands and their protection was included. That law charges both the EPA and the Army Corps of Engineers with the legal responsibility to protect wetlands. On the other hand, lobbyists for agricultural interests, oil companies, mining concerns, and land development have a long history of pushing to have wetlands "redefined" so they can use them for their own purposes.

The question of definition is extremely important because it means the difference between protection and loss. By 1994 a revised federal ruling on the matter is expected.

Half of our wetlands on the mainland USA have already been sacrificed to urban development, agriculture, flood control, and industry, and the fate of those in Alaska is in the hands of our legislators. Each year an estimated 300,000 to 500,000 additional acres of wetlands are eliminated. Those remaining affect the quality of life and the future of fresh water, even if they are within another state's boundaries.

The Arkansas River is an example of an ecological need currently competing with other fresh-water demands. The Arkansas used to be the longest continuous **tributary** to the Mississippi, winding and twisting 1,459 miles through Colorado, Kansas, Oklahoma, and Arkansas. It roared through the Royal Gorge, then provided water for wetlands, valleys, and fertile plains where wildlife such as trout, beaver, ducks, bald eagles, elk, buffalo, and bears found a safe refuge. Cities and industries sprang up along its shores. Now those very cities and industries have brought this once great river to its knees as it fights to be a river as well as an important and valuable fresh-water resource.

In Europe, another well-known river, the "beautiful blue Danube," is in a struggle for survival. Most of it is no longer blue or beautiful, but once upon a time it was a major ecological environment for humans, plants, and wildlife. It sustained a large river basin and a fertile forest, and recharged underground reservoirs. Then it was dammed to provide water for hydroelectrical power. Eighty percent of the river's 400-mile stretch through Austria is blocked by a series of nine hydropower plants.

The demand for Danube water reached a point where a new proposal for yet another dam finally diverted the river into a concrete canal. A section of the canal was completed before public outcry resulted in Hungary withdrawing from its part of the contract. What is now Slovakia has taken the case to the World Court in The Hague where the battle for the waters of the Danube continues.

Two factors that affect shortages and competition are **droughts** and seasonal demand. Periodic droughts come about when rainfall is below normal for several years in a row. They can be the result of El Nino, a complex interaction of winds, currents, and sea temperatures. In recent years, El Nino brought more southerly winds, which carry less rainfall, to North and South America, Australia, New Zealand, and the Pacific. In New Zealand, the resulting drought limited the production of the south island's hydroelectrical facilities where 70 percent of the nation's power is produced. New Zealand Limited had to ask all its customers, including those industries most important to the nation's economy, to cut back electrical usage. Meteorologists say there must be the return of westerly winds before a normally moist climate can be expected.

Droughts are particularly hard on arid regions, such as the southwestern United States, but they also affect areas that usually have adequate or abundant rainfall. Oklahoma's adequate supply of surface and groundwater did not protect residents from the Dust Bowl crisis of the early 1930s, when drought and unrestricted agricultural practices combined to force thousands of people to migrate westward. Droughts still strike Oklahoma and cause extended shortages even though the state now has advanced water and soil conservation programs that cushion the most severe effects.

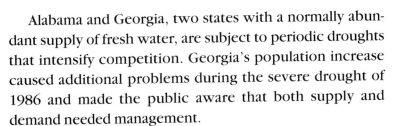

Run only full loads in the washing machine and dishwasher. Cutting down on the number of loads you do will save 75 to 200 gallons a week. Also, use a bucket, not a hose, to wash the car or your bike. This will save 50 gallons per wash.

Alabama and Georgia, two states with a normally abundant supply of fresh water, are subject to periodic droughts that intensify competition. Georgia's population increase caused additional problems during the severe drought of 1986 and made the public aware that both supply and demand needed management.

Seasonal demands heighten shortages and competition when an influx of tourists swells a state's population. Nevada, the most arid state in the nation and one that is subject to droughts, also has to cope with meeting the demands of a great number of visitors. Fifty-nine percent of Nevadans live in the Las Vegas area, which is also the prime destina-

tion of tourists who flock there, particularly in the winter months.

Hawaii, the state with the greatest number of inches of annual rainfall in the nation, frequently finds its resources stretched beyond the limit by tourists. In the city of Honolulu, on the island of Oahu, seasonal resident demand already exceeds supply. Oahu has a nearly ideal system of water resources, yet it has Hawaii's most serious water supply problems. By the year 2020, local shortages have been projected for three areas of Oahu, where 77 percent of the Hawaiian residents live, and for one area of Maui. It is ironic that this state, with an average 70 inches of rainfall a year, should have such an imbalance in availability and demand, and in population growth and distribution, that fresh-water shortages and competition should cloud its traditional "Aloha!" to all who visit its shores.

Chapter Three

Pollution—

A Deadly

Enemy

ONE FACTOR HAS SUCH AN IMPORTANT EFFECT ON BOTH SHORTAGES and competition for fresh-water resources that it deserves separate consideration. That factor is pollution. When water becomes contaminated—no matter how much of it is available—it is no longer fit or safe for human or animal use.

It should be noted that enough federal laws have been passed in recent years to prevent further pollution and to clean up existing waste disposal sites. One reason the enforcement of those laws is painfully slow is the cost factor. Federal funds are no longer readily available. For the private sector to assume the cost of cleanup and of making the production and disposal changes needed to comply with federal regulations would in many cases put farmers, industries, commerce, and cities out of business, and cause economic havoc.

The quality of fresh water became an issue when the public was alerted to the fact that pollution was a threat to health. Fishermen were one of the first groups to sound an alarm. Suddenly they realized that our oceans, lakes, rivers, ponds, marshes, streams, and the ground itself was being polluted with wastewater carrying all sorts of foreign substances, some of them deadly poisons. Rivers noted for their salmon runs, popular trout streams, and lakes were almost devoid of fish. Worse yet, the fish that were caught turned out to be tainted with disease-causing chemicals. Environmental awareness had reached the grass roots of America.

It didn't take long for the fishermen to be heard. Other segments of the population started to complain. People began to suspect that their drinking water was not worth drinking anymore. It might even contain substances that caused deadly diseases. By the early 1900s, epidemics of serious waterborne diseases in California, Massachusetts, and New York resulted in a national study of drinking water quality. Fear of pollution made the headlines.

Health officials found that by adding chlorine to the public water supply it could be disinfected, putting an end to that scare. A few years later, tests showed that chlorine combines with organic matter in the water and forms a class of compounds known as **trihalomethanes**, simply called **THMs**. Further tests uncovered the fact that THMs could be cancer causing. The alarm caused by that report brought about the Safe Drinking Water Act and eventually a solution to the threat of THMs was found. Today public water supplies are carefully monitored and pollution is fresh water's "public enemy number one."

Who is responsible for water pollution? Every segment of society shares the blame. To use water is to expose it to some degree of pollution. As a rule, the major water users are also the major water polluters. They cause contamination either directly through **point sources** such as landfills, industrial dumps, and treated sewage disposal, or indirectly through **nonpoint sources** such as runoff from farmlands, city streets, storm drains, feedlots, construction sites, and mines. Neither point nor nonpoint pollution is legally acceptable any longer.

Farmers apply fertilizers and pesticides to their fields in order to keep the acres they irrigate highly productive. Plant growth absorbs most of these additives, but what isn't

absorbed becomes part of the runoff that seeps into the soil of nearby ponds and streams. The percentage that becomes runoff may be small, but when such great amounts of chemicals are added the pollution that results is no small matter. In one year, 1987, in one state, Nebraska, 775,000 tons of fertilizers and 16,550 tons of pesticides were used on farms and ranches, while livestock contributed 235,000 tons of manure.

Ideally, the toxic chemicals that contaminate water are filtered out as the runoff passes through layers of ground cover, roots, soil, gravel, and rock. The combined action of soil filtering and plant **osmosis**, which means diffusion through the living membranes, is the most efficient and natural way to remove impurities before they can seep into surface or groundwater resources.

The capacity of this natural filtering system can fail if more waste than it can handle is dumped at one time. When that happens, the toxic seepage turns up in fresh-water supplies. Groundwater is most vulnerable to toxic seepage because water's natural movement is influenced by the force of gravity and is generally downward. And since irrigation is so widespread and has been practiced for centuries without regard to what was happening underground, its effects on water quality in some groundwater basins are critical.

One specific global effect of irrigation is the **salinization**, or salting, of soil. Salt deposits build up when fields become waterlogged because of poor drainage or because of the common practice of overwatering. As standing water evaporates, salt is **leached** out of the soil and deposited on the surface, making the fields useless as far as crop production is concerned. Sometimes many acres of good quality

cropland are "salted up" when the water used for irrigation contains salts. Salinization is such a problem that it is reducing the world's crop production by an estimated 24 percent based on the top five international irrigators, India, China, the United States, Pakistan, and the Commonwealth of Independent States.

Another form of water pollution caused by agriculture is the high **selenium** concentration found in runoff. Irrigation washes more selenium out of the soil in a short time than centuries of natural rainfall. While a very small amount of this natural element is needed by humans and some animals, concentrations of it are extremely poisonous and are hazardous to wildlife and possibly to humans.

Twenty-two wildlife areas have been found to contain high concentrations of selenium. The pollution in Kesterson National Wildlife Refuge in California has earned it the title of "Three Mile Island of irrigated agriculture." Other sites showing potentially lethal contamination are the Tulare Basin, also in California; Stillwater National Refuge, Nevada; Ouray National Wildlife Refuge, Utah; and the Kendrick Project in Wyoming.

Urban and suburban residents and businesses contribute to the problem of pollution by producing a staggering amount of garbage and wastewater, both of which are difficult and costly to dispose of safely. For years the public had an "out of sight, out of mind" attitude regarding household or commercial waste. Once it was learned that drinking water quality is linked to how such waste is disposed of, both the public and officials took a hard look at the methods of disposal.

What they saw was a general pattern of inefficient and incomplete waste treatment that even today has not been

WATER SAVER

Keep a bottle of water in the
refrigerator for drinking. Not turning on
the faucet each time you need a drink
will save 200 to 300 gallons a week.

entirely corrected. Some wastewater treatment plants are
still poorly designed or inadequate, or both. When they
break down or are overloaded, untreated sewage is sometimes dumped directly into oceans, lakes, or rivers. All sorts
of microbiological contaminants as well as organic and inorganic chemicals that are not removed during the treatment
process can potentially become part of the public supply of
drinking water.

After years of careless dumping, the Delaware River had
such a high chemical content that it could "eat the paint off
of ships." Today, the Delaware is relatively clean, but the
cost of cleanup is so high and so many sites need cleaning
that it is a major national burden.

Muskegon County, Michigan, on the eastern shore of
Lake Michigan, completed a pilot project 20 years ago that is
a model for water districts trying to avoid what happened to
the Delaware River. The wastewater is treated and reused to

irrigate about 5,500 acres of normally unproductive sandy soil. The crops of corn, soybeans, and alfalfa that are grown are part of the natural filtering system that makes use of the misplaced nutrients in the wastewater. They add as much as $1 million per season to the Muskegon economy. They also improve the water quality of three inland lakes, making them fit for recreational use and contributing to the area's prosperity.

An even older pilot program that serves as a model for avoiding cleanup costs is Lubbock, Texas. As early as the 1930s, the city used treated sewage water to irrigate land that served to pasture horses and milk cows, and to grow a variety of grains, all successfully. Natural filtering returned the water to the Ogallala aquifer, recharging it as much as ten feet a year. Eventually, Lubbock's wastewater reuse developed into the Canyon Lakes Project that became a Texas-size recreational oasis. Now, 25 years later, it is still an exception to the state's chronic lack of water and to the usual dilemma of wastewater treatment.

Careless wastewater disposal is what polluted Boston Harbor, which is now undergoing a more than $6 billion cleanup. As part of that ambitious program, the Massachusetts Water Resources Authority (MWRA) is operating a fertilizer plant using sludge from two sewage treatment plants to produce black soil-like pellets. The plant is a key factor in the city's effort to stop the discharge of up to 500,000 gallons of sewage wastewater into the Harbor that has been going on for 40 years. The "sludge cake" is mixed with synthetic nutrients to form a fertilizer that is then sold out of state to help pay for the cleanup. MWRA's goal is to produce 65,000 dry tons of pellets by 1998.

Making fertilizer pellets out of sludge is not a new idea.

Milwaukee, Wisconsin, has been doing it for almost 70 years. So have other cities all over the United States. But applying it to the cleanup of Boston Harbor is a novel way to reverse the disastrous result of waterway discharge.

Garbage disposal is no less a major and costly burden, both nationally and internationally. The United States alone produces well over 100 million tons of garbage each year. Cities are virtual garbage factories, with domestic and commercial sources contributing the largest part. Garbage trucks used to pick up trash cans and haul them as far away and out of sight as possible, usually where the trash could be set on fire to reduce the bulk. The remainder was bulldozed and used for landfills without first making certain that dump sites were not located where the contaminating seepage would end up in a groundwater resource. In the United States, garbage disposal is now being regulated and made relatively safe by first lining dump sites with impermeable material, but there are countless abandoned dumps and old landfills that continue to contribute to groundwater pollution.

While leaders from all over the world were at the Earth Summit in Brazil talking about the future of our planet, the city of Rio de Janeiro was staggering under its own garbage summit. Rio de Janeiro has a population of nine million and produces 10,000 tons of trash a day. It has one state-of-the-art processing plant that can handle about 1,200 tons every 24 hours. The remainder piles up in dumps in and around the city. The runoff and seepage into Guanabara Bay is out of control. At one of the largest dumps, the Gramacho landfill, upward of 2,000 people live off the trash, recycling it, reusing it, eating it. Their exposure to unhealthy conditions is also out of control. Three more processing plants are

planned, paid for by international funds, but nothing is being done to clean up the water pollution the dumps are causing. So while diplomats looked at problems on a world scale, they may well have overlooked their host city's environmental crisis.

Lead is probably the most common drinking water contaminant and also the most harmful. Young children and infants appear to be highly vulnerable to lead poisoning. It is a type of pollution that is literally "built-in" and to which the public is being exposed on a daily basis without being aware of it.

Exposure takes place in homes and commercial buildings through plumbing systems that were installed using lead solder, flux, and piping. The reaction between the water and the lead results in a leaching process that contaminates the flow of water drawn from the tap. Federal law now bans the use of lead products in new installations, but locating and replacing those in previously built homes and businesses is a complicated process. The danger of lead poisoning can be greatly minimized by not cooking with or drinking water from the hot water tap and by flushing the cold water faucet before drawing water if it has not been used in six hours.

The manufacturing and processing plants operated by industry and mining to produce the goods that are part of the high standard of living in the United States also produce one trillion pounds of hazardous waste a year. How to dispose of such an enormous amount of waste safely is one of the major problems faced by both industry and mining in this decade.

Over the years, waste material was dumped into surface impoundments such as landfills, pits, ponds, and lagoons.

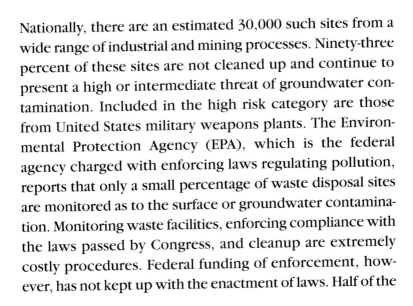

Water lawns and flowers only at dusk or
early in the morning. This way more of
the water is used and not evaporated.
Covering your swimming pool when it's
not in use will prevent 1,300 gallons
from evaporating.

Nationally, there are an estimated 30,000 such sites from a
wide range of industrial and mining processes. Ninety-three
percent of these sites are not cleaned up and continue to
present a high or intermediate threat of groundwater contamination. Included in the high risk category are those
from United States military weapons plants. The Environmental Protection Agency (EPA), which is the federal
agency charged with enforcing laws regulating pollution,
reports that only a small percentage of waste disposal sites
are monitored as to the surface or groundwater contamination. Monitoring waste facilities, enforcing compliance with
the laws passed by Congress, and cleanup are extremely
costly procedures. Federal funding of enforcement, however, has not kept up with the enactment of laws. Half of the

land disposal sites are considered by the EPA to be in violation, and 378,000 industrial and business concerns are still granted exemptions from federal regulations.

In addition to surface impoundments, industrial wastes such as organic solvents, corrosives, brines, reactive, and radioactive materials are disposed of by underground injection into deep and shallow wells, abandoned mines, or aquifers containing nonpotable water. Because restrictions on surface disposal were upgraded in recent years, industry started using more deep well disposals. Now ten billion gallons of waste a year are flushed out of sight this way.

Another method of disposal that dates back to the beginning of civilization is to discharge the waste into rivers or streams. The theory behind this practice is that "dilution is the solution to pollution." Even though the theory has been proved wrong, discharge into waterways is still being done by industry as well as other water users. When several users discharge waste into the same waterway, the result can be disastrous.

The case of Pralls Island located in the Arthur Kill Channel between New York City and New Jersey is an example. The 88-acre island is inhabited by flocks of rare birds that use its wetlands as feeding and nesting grounds. Their safety is threatened by waste disposal from an oil refinery and other industries, and from what seems to be the largest garbage dump in the world.

In 1991 several oil spills, including one involving 567,000 gallons from a ruptured underwater Exxon pipeline, decimated the flocks' food supply and exposed them to toxins. Exxon agreed to pay for a restoration project on Pralls Island, but it may take decades before the wetlands can support the marine and bird population dependent on it.

Spills are only one way the petroleum industry contributes to pollution. Abandoned oil wells found by the thousands, particularly throughout Oklahoma and Texas, present another threat of contamination. An abandoned well seeps waste oil while it acts as a pipeline allowing salt water to find its way into fresh-water aquifers. The Texas Railroad Commission estimates that it may cost $300 million to plug that one state's unused oil wells.

To a pollution-conscious public, "heavy metal" is not a type of music. It is a specific type of industrial contamination that is showing up in public water supplies and fresh-water resources. A growing number are found to have unsafe levels of heavy metals such as lead, mercury, asbestos, dioxin, arsenic, and cyanide, making them unfit for use as drinking water. Dioxin, which is a by-product of the bleaching process used in pulp and paper mills, was the chemical that caused the evacuation of Love Canal in New York State and Times Beach in Missouri.

Acid rain, defined as chemically polluted rainfall, is caused in part by industry's coal-burning plants. When water molecules combine with the sulfur dioxide emitted by the burning of coal, and with nitrogen oxide from auto emissions, the result is an acidity very harmful to fish, wildlife, plants, and trees. According to some researchers, whole forests and large lakes are currently at risk. Already, 1,200 lakes in the United States have been completely acidified. This means that the lake water is unfit for human use and that little can live in it. The same fate threatens 40 percent of our nation's wild trout streams.

The eastern United States and Canada are especially vulnerable to acid rain, which is blamed for the loss of millions of dollars in recreational fishing alone. Canada is pressuring

the United States to do something about the fallout they get from sources within our borders. Doing something means that the American public has to be willing to use less electricity, cut down on coal-burning power generation, drive their cars less, and use public transportation and car pools more in order to reduce auto emissions. This would take a change in life-style, which is not a politically popular subject.

Meanwhile the United States is pressuring Canada to do something about the millions of gallons of untreated sewage being disposed of by the city of Victoria into the waters between Vancouver Island and the Olympic Peninsula, and also the toxic chemical waste dumped by Canadian government agencies and industries, which ends up in the Columbia and Fraser rivers. Because of the latter practice, the state of Washington has had to issue a warning about possible fish contamination. Such international problems of pollution are not uncommon where neighboring countries share an aquatic border.

Pollution problems are particularly acute in other highly industrialized countries like Korea, which in recent years has been trying to catch up with the United States and other advanced nations. In 1989 high concentrations of heavy metals were found in the Han River that runs through the city of Seoul. More recently, an electronics manufacturing plant in South Korea was alleged to have dumped 30 tons of phenol, a dangerous chemical, into the Naakong River upstream of what is a fresh-water source for ten million people and a wildlife sanctuary. Fortunately, phenol has an extremely obnoxious odor that alerted residents to the health threat as soon as they turned on their water taps.

These two incidents, and another involving THMs found

Hold a family meeting and share what you have learned about water conservation with the other members of your family. Together, you can save thousands of gallons a month.

in Seoul's drinking water, resulted in such adverse publicity that Korea's Environmental Bureau was raised to the status of a ministry. Utility officials are now forced to analyze drinking water quality daily rather than monthly to protect against further industrial pollution.

Mining has a long history of contributing to pollution but new methods of extracting valuable metals, minerals, and coal have compounded the problem. The longwall system, which is a modern technique for the extraction of coal, is causing widespread concern in Appalachia and other mining areas in the West and Midwest. Coal companies claim it is the most efficient and safe mining method, but residents and environmentalists are worried about the system's devastating effects, causing the **subsidence**, or sinking, of land, rechanneling of springs, draining of wells, and disruption of

groundwater resources. The conflict pits environmental concerns against the economy, which may come down to saving miners' jobs versus saving a stream or aquifer.

Nuclear power plants generate 20 percent of our nation's electricity and 90 percent of its radioactive waste. Just as noxious waste is the product of nuclear reactors, public alarm is the product of the spills and leaks that have plagued the industry. The nuclear community has to find a safe way to dispose of radioactive waste if the public is to eventually feel secure about the 110 reactors now in operation in the United States.

A few nuclear plants in the United States, France, and England have successful waste disposal, reprocessing, and storage programs, but these successes are overshadowed by incidents of traumatic failure. Because no new plants have been built since 1974, the life of existing facilities is being extended. There is no guarantee that old nuclear plants continue to be at least as safe as when they were built. Watchdog groups such as the Union of Concerned Scientists are pressing for a fail-proof solution to nuclear waste disposal.

Until all major users do a better job of literally "cleaning up their act," pollution will no doubt be a contributing factor in national and international fresh-water shortages and competition for a long time to come.

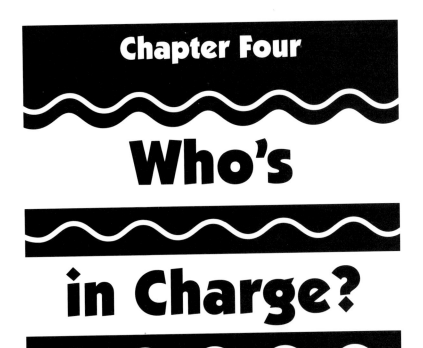

Chapter Four

Who's

in Charge?

WHO MANAGES OUR NATIONAL WATER RESOURCES? WHO DECIDES which users should win in the competition for fresh water?

Early American settlers followed the English law that gave landowners absolute freedom to use and allocate the surface or groundwater on their property. Since then, variations of this absolute doctrine have evolved in the courts to provide for private and public needs under state and federal management systems.

State agencies such as the Office of State Engineer, the Department of Natural Resources and Environmental Control, and the Water Conservation Board play primary roles in allocating fresh-water resources, granting and regulating rights, and administering the business of water distribution for the benefit of the general public. Their authority then filters down to a number of local agencies such as water districts, irrigation districts, and county water authorities. Administration varies from state to state, but the functions they oversee include withdrawing, supplying, distributing, and treating the public supply, imposing water conservation measures, making local water exchanges, supervising water quality, and collecting and treating wastewater. These duties are performed according to state and federal regulations. All state laws must at least meet the requirements of federal law but may impose more strict standards.

Although most of the responsibility for the allocation and management of fresh-water resources rests with each state, the federal government continues to play a substantial role.

First of all, congressional representatives are the lawmakers. They have the constitutional responsibility to enter into treaties with Canada and Mexico concerning water management. They have "reserved water rights" for certain public lands. They are responsible for treaties and agreements with Native Americans.

In addition, federal agencies control massive projects such as the Tennessee Valley Authority and the Bureau of Reclamation's Central Valley Project in California. Federal courts take part in settling disputes over such things as interstate contracts. In most other matters of water management, the federal government's present role is secondary to those of the state.

There was a period during the mid-20th century, however, when federal agencies had a more expansive authority regarding fresh-water resources through the construction and management of large, government-sponsored projects. In order to encourage the settling of the West, thereby turning it into productive cropland, the federal government established a **reclamation** service that later became the Bureau of Reclamation. It took over the funding and building of dams and reservoirs, land-drainage systems, and aqueduct projects to carry out the policy of western expansion designed to benefit the entire nation. To help achieve quick results, the bureau started subsidizing agricultural development by providing irrigation water to farmers at less than full cost.

During the 1970s, public awareness of the cost of these massive federal projects, and the possible negative effects on the environment of further water development, brought expansion to a virtual halt. Since then, the role of the Bureau of Reclamation has changed somewhat. The West has been

in a period of transition from water supply development to water demand management and conservation.

Federal policy now requires that local and regional agencies, and those specific users who benefit directly or indirectly from a water project, share in the cost of planning and construction in order to get federal funds. In addition, even though the secretary of the interior is continuing to renew most long-term low-cost contracts as they come up for renewal, the Bureau of Reclamation is moving toward modifying its long-standing agricultural subsidies by increasing the cost of irrigation water to a price closer to its actual value.

These changes, combined with recent water shortages and increased competition, have made fresh-water resources the hottest things on the market. The cost of water is beginning to determine how it is allocated. The state's responsibility where both allocation and rights are concerned is being increased. A new federal/state partnership is evolving.

Both state and federal agencies are involved in the matter of water rights, a complicated tangle of old and new doctrines. Individual states have their own variations and mixtures of these doctrines. In the arid West, for instance, the chronic shortage of fresh water made water wars a common occurrence and influenced the evolution of the basic principles on which present doctrines are based.

The oldest and most widely adopted doctrine concerning surface water rights is known as **prior appropriation**. That term grew out of the western claim of "first in time, first in right." According to this doctrine, whoever first uses a water resource for a beneficial purpose has senior rights to it. If there is enough water for another user or users, they

can be granted junior, or secondary, rights as long as these do not interfere with the original user's allotted share.

Another basic surface water right is known as the "**riparian reasonable use**" doctrine, which holds that someone who owns land adjoining a surface water resource or through whose property such a resource flows, has a right to use it. A riparian right cannot be impaired in quality or diminished in quantity by upstream users. Neither does it give the landowner the right to waste the water or use it in a way that adversely affects other upstream or downstream users.

The doctrine governing groundwater rights works differently. A landowner may have absolute rights to use for beneficial purposes a water resource located under his property to the depth of the center of the earth. He may have instead the right of reasonable use of that resource as needed to maintain his property. Or he may have only correlative rights, which are shared with other landowners drawing from a common underground source.

A dramatic 1992 ruling by David Pope, chief engineer of the Division of Water Resources for the state of Kansas, set a policy of "**sustainable yield**," which directly affects water rights. Sustainable yield means that the amount of water withdrawn from a resource can be limited regardless of rights if that amount cannot be sustained. The Pope decision came in the case of Cheyenne Bottoms, a 20,000 acre refuge for migratory birds that has been designated as a "Wetlands of International Importance." The decision recognizes wetlands water rights along with those of agriculture. It is the first time a state has given consideration to the long-term availability of water for an ecological need on a par with a short-term use for irrigation of farmlands. The only other

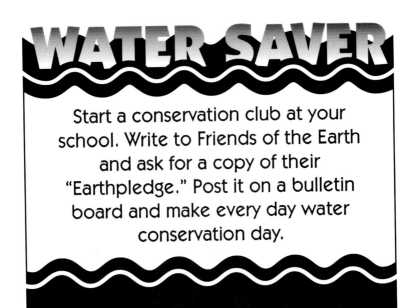

Start a conservation club at your school. Write to Friends of the Earth and ask for a copy of their "Earthpledge." Post it on a bulletin board and make every day water conservation day.

sustainable yield ruling by a state was made in Arizona in 1980, but this gave agricultural interests 25 years to comply. Pope's decision took effect immediately and is expected to set a precedent for other similar water disputes.

The history of the case goes back to 1948 when the state's Department of Wildlife and Parks was granted rights to divert over 16 billion gallons of water a year from the Arkansas River and Wet Walnut Creek to preserve Cheyenne Bottoms, then thought of mainly as a prime duck-hunting area. For years farmers also drew water directly from the creek until the flow began to decrease. Then in the 1960s and 1970s, farmers sank 524 irrigation wells, pumping from the alluvial valley to fill their growing needs. It wasn't long before Wet Walnut Creek was no longer wet.

With the Arkansas River in western Kansas also dry for

long stretches of time, the Bottoms hit bottom. In the summer of 1989, the combined withdrawal of the irrigation wells and a two-year drought caused the wetlands to dry up. "When the shorebirds arrived on their northward migration route," reports the Wichita *Eagle*, "the invertebrate cupboard was bare."

The Kansas Department of Wildlife and Parks complained that since 1980, Cheyenne Bottoms had been getting less than 10 percent of the water to which it held senior rights. They blamed the loss of water on the farmers' increased withdrawal. They were told by the Board of Agriculture that they had to prove their claim. This was the standard answer given to all complaints filed by senior water rights holders. The state had obviously allocated more water than it could deliver, and in the minds of officials the farmers came first as they always had.

But the state's Division of Water Resources supported the wildlife agency's claim, stating that since the 1960s, the aquifer that is the source of water in that area sustained about a 30 percent decline. In addition, the Soil Conservation Service, another federal agency, cited the farmers' irrigation as the cause for the drying up of Wet Walnut Creek.

Finally, under threat of a public lawsuit if they didn't do something to reclaim water rights for Cheyenne Bottoms, the Kansas Department of Wildlife and Parks conducted a two-year study that again put the blame squarely on the shoulders of the farmers. They asked that enough wells be shut down to allow the aquifer to completely recharge within seven years.

The struggle to find a solution involved just about every emotional, economical, and legal aspect of every water problem found in every other state. In the end, the fate of

Cheyenne Bottoms came to rest in the hands of one person, the chief engineer of water resources. Years ago, when it first became apparent that the state had allocated more water rights than it could deliver, the State Legislature empowered the chief engineer to supersede water rights granted under prior appropriation and to reallocate them as he or she saw fit. It should be noted that the chief engineer is appointed by the secretary of agriculture, who is appointed by the State Board of Agriculture, which is named by the farm lobby, an unusual one-sided arrangement.

"Where does that leave Cheyenne Bottoms?" the public asked. Ninety percent of the world's population of five shorebird species pass through these wetlands on their migration route through the interior of the United States. In addition, hundreds of thousands of ducks and geese, and thousands of sandhill cranes, blue herons, and the endangered whooping crane depend on the marshland to feed and rest before taking off for the Arctic tundra. If Cheyenne Bottoms was lost, the birds would have no place else to go for their migratory break.

On one side of the competition were farmers like Margaret Oborney quoted in the Wichita *Eagle* as saying, "Without our irrigation, or with a drastic cut, there is very little chance of continuing our family farm." On the other side were concerned citizens like Alan Wentz quoted in the same issue of the Wichita *Eagle* as saying, "This isn't a question of whether farming is more important than birds, it's a question of who has the earliest rights."

The surprise ruling by chief engineer David Pope ordered Great Bend farmers to reduce their irrigation by almost 50 percent, depending on if individual rights were granted before or after 1948. In addition, some cities and

industries in the area were cut back 10 percent in order to increase the future flow into the wetlands. Even while wildlife organizations were hailing the Cheyenne Bottoms decision as timely and farsighted, farmers wasted no time fighting it in court. A few hours after the Pope ruling was made public, two groups of irrigators filed a lawsuit challenging the state's authority to restrict their water rights. Eventually a compromise agreement delayed the most severe cutbacks for a year. This gave farmers flexibility to plan necessary crop changes. For the time being at least, an important wetlands has been granted the water resources it needs for survival.

Another issue that is being hammered out in the courts involves **water transfers** or **water marketing**, which has been described as the transfer of water rights "between willing buyers and sellers for an agreed-upon price." The principal question is if water should be treated as a natural resource or as a commodity to be bought and sold. At stake is whether farmers or other users who hold rights to great amounts of water have the option to transfer those rights to another user willing to pay a fair market price for an increased supply. Because water shortages are not expected to go away, this practice is being considered as probably the most reasonable way to meet growing urban and industrial demands, particularly in the arid West.

Each western state has its own variation of laws regulating water transfers. In Arizona, neither state agencies nor the courts encourage the practice. California, on the other hand, encourages and smooths the way for voluntary transfers that serve to reallocate the state's water resources to meet specific needs. Colorado law favors transfers and treats water rights the same as property rights. They can be

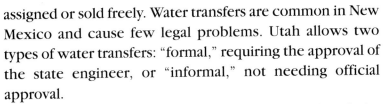

Find out if your school recycles. Not wasting paper will cut down on the number of trees that are cut down, protecting the earth's water storage system. If your school doesn't have a recycling program, find out how you can start one.

assigned or sold freely. Water transfers are common in New Mexico and cause few legal problems. Utah allows two types of water transfers: "formal," requiring the approval of the state engineer, or "informal," not needing official approval.

Both state and federal agencies are concerned with the question of ethics as well as with laws and rights regarding water transfers. Because irrigation represents such large amounts of water, farmers are logical targets for cities willing to pay a high price for it. Farmers therefore stand to make more profit selling water than by using it to grow crops. But is it ethical for a farmer to sell water for more than the federally subsidized price he was charged?

The profit factor is a complicated one that has to evolve with the value of water. To some extent, water marketing in one form or another has been going on for years and proves that "water seeks its own economic level." As long as increased demand continues to place a higher value on limited supply, water transfers and marketing will be used as tools to bring about a more practical distribution of resources.

What happens when a state boundary is involved in a water transfer or rights dispute? Water resources don't stop when they reach a state line. Both surface and groundwater are often located so they are available for withdrawal in two or more states at the same time. Who, then, owns the water? Can a farmer use his water rights in one state to water his acreage located in a neighboring state?

Several interstate groundwater management groups have been formed to help deal with multistate problems. The Delaware River Basin Commission and the Susquehanna River Basin Commission were established by both state and federal law for that purpose. They cooperate with other agencies in the states involved and regulate permits for projects within the particular river basin that they serve.

A landmark case, known as *Sporhase v. Nebraska,* that involved an interstate dispute over water rights, went all the way to the United States Supreme Court for a final decision. The ruling, handed down in 1982, determined that water is an article of interstate commerce protected by a clause in the United States Constitution. Therefore state boundaries alone can no longer be a basis for preventing the interstate transfer of water if it is needed elsewhere for beneficial use.

The *Sporhase* decision opened the door as far as a state's absolute ownership of its water resources is concerned. It is

having an impact on cases like the current dispute between Texas and New Mexico involving 326 well permit applications filed by residents of the water-poor city of El Paso to withdraw water from a water-rich groundwater basin just across the New Mexico state line.

There is no area of federal responsibility today that is more critical and controversial than the growing number of claims by Indian tribes to water they feel should be theirs. To the Bureau of Indian Affairs and other federal agencies, the question of Indian water rights is a moral and legal obligation that can no longer be put off. To the states involved, it is a matter of possibly losing control of a portion of an already limited supply of water. To the Indian tribes, it means restoring their dignity as "original nations of America" and ensuring economic and social independence.

Michael J. Clinton, with the Department of the Interior, gave a clear picture of the Indians' need for water when he said, "An Indian reservation without water is like an automobile without gasoline—maybe you can live in it, but it isn't going to take you anywhere."

The Indian tribes' legal right to water was decided by the Supreme Court in *Winters v. United States* in 1906, in which reservation rights were upheld as the implied intent of Congress. In accord with the doctrine of prior appropriation, the tribes' use of water resources was predominantly first in time so it is first in right. The question left unanswered concerns quantity. How much water do those federally established "Winters rights" reserve for Indian tribes?

In *Arizona v. California* in 1963, the Supreme Court set the only standard to date regarding quantity by granting five lower Colorado River Indian reservations enough water needed for the "practicable irrigable acreage" within their

boundaries. The Court did not specify exactly how much that amount should be, nor did it declare that the standard set in that case applied to other Indian claims.

There are almost 80 cases currently in court in western states involving Indians' reserved rights. Every one of the cases pending involves unquantified Winters rights. Without a national standard for quantification, it is difficult, if not impossible, for the western states to carry out effective water conservation and management programs. In Arizona, for example, tribes may have reserved rights to more irrigation water than the state can reasonably allot.

Several federal agencies are involved in the effort to settle the claims of these original nations of America through negotiation. The Department of the Interior has established guidelines and a working group to represent federal interests and responsibilities. On the other hand, the National Congress of American Indians issued a paper claiming each Indian nation's sovereign prerogative to set its own priorities regarding its unique water rights, plans, laws, and needs, some of which may not be negotiated. If negotiation fails, then settlement of claims will rest on litigation. Both are lengthy and costly processes that will ultimately effect the competition for water resources in the West and in our entire nation.

Indians' rights have been called the "wild card" in the current dispute over the allocation of the Missouri River. Indian reservations were slighted when the Army Corps of Engineers built its six main dams on the river that was once the gateway to the West. Now the corps is being sued by three states, South Dakota, North Dakota, and Montana, which say that the present system of distributing the Missouri's water is unfair and outdated. They want the corps to

Find out who is in charge of the water treatment plant in your area. See if your teacher can arrange a field trip to visit the plant. Ask what is being done about wastewater reclamation in your area.

give recreational needs a higher priority over such things as barge traffic on the river. Indian tribes are hoping that if the suit results in changes in federal policy, they will end up with their rightful share of water. The quantity that could be awarded to Indian tribes is enormous. The Indians who once had this river all to themselves may become the future water brokers in the marketing of the Missouri's flow.

There are many users waiting for the outcome of this court battle. Irrigation needs, energy projects, out-of-basin water transfers, walleye survival, and states' rights are competing along with Indian tribes. Upstream states are battling against downstream neighbors. The Missouri is one of the

West's and Midwest's last unapportioned waterways of consequence. Its flow is subject to drought and pollution. Now it is subject to a fight that could take years to settle.

If interstate allocation is complicated, international agreements are even more so. Egypt's water supply comes almost entirely from the Nile River, which does not originate within the nation's boundaries. Nine countries draw from the Nile River basin, with Egypt at the end of the line. The river's water is impounded by the Aswân High Dam, forming Lake Nasser, which serves as a reservoir. Eighty percent of the lake's water comes from the Blue Nile, which forms in Ethiopia. Twenty percent is from the White Nile, with headwaters in Tanzania.

Under an agreement with Sudan, where both forks of the Niles meet, Egypt was allotted two-thirds of the flow entering the Aswân Dam on an average year. But the agreement between Egypt and the Sudan made back in 1959 is not recognized by Ethiopia as a permanent and absolute right. Ethiopia's plans for future development of its own could have drastic consequences on the Blue Nile's flow at the Sudan border. They would cut into Egypt's water supply and add to the national crisis caused by its population growth.

As with most matters dealing with fresh-water resources, there are other factors that muddy the waters. The Sudan/Egyptian allotment was based on the average yearly flow into the Aswân, and did not take into account that the Nile has frequent subaverage years. Droughts have severe effects on the river's flow. A dry period in 1984–1985 brought it down even below the share allotted to Egypt. In the fall of 1986, Lake Nasser was still down to one-fifth of the dam's capacity. Since then, heavy rainfall has restored the

reservoir, but the relief could be only temporary. The Nile has a 100-year cycle, with dry periods occurring at the beginning of every century. A better system of international water management can't be delayed much longer.

Better water management would have avoided the shrinking of the Aral Sea in Soviet Central Asia, which was once the fourth largest body of fresh water on earth, with a surface area of nearly 250,000 square miles. It is now half that size and is expected to completely disappear by early in the next century. The Aral Sea's slow but sure shrinkage is caused by years of diverting excessive water from the Syr Darya and Amu Darya rivers, the two main streams that flow into it, causing the rivers themselves to virtually dry up and leaving the sea without a water source.

Tens of thousands of workers lost jobs in the Aral Sea fisheries and were forced to leave when a decline in fish stock drove them out of business. Residents who have remained are exposed to poor drinking water quality which is affecting their health. They watch helplessly while salt deposits blowing off the former seabed destroy surrounding croplands. Water authorities expect there will have to be a 60 percent cutback in irrigation of the cotton, rice, fruit, and vegetables which provide food and jobs for the masses.

The Syr Darya and Amu Darya rivers now pass through four of the five newly independent nations of Kazakhstan, Kyrygyzstan, Tajikistan, Turkmenistan, and Uzbekistan. All of these countries are mainly agricultural and depend on the rivers for 75 percent of their water. That includes agricultural production, as well as drinking water and sanitation for a growing population of 52 million people. The prospect of conflicts over water rights and unsettled boundaries makes

water management seem impossible. The breaking up of the Soviet Union may well have been the final blow that sealed the Aral Sea's fate.

Sandra Postel, senior researcher at Worldwatch Institute, in Washington, D.C., writes in a recent report that, "Soviet Central Asia by no means rounds out the list of the world's water problem areas. The Valley of Mexico, much of northern and eastern Africa, the American West, pockets of Eastern Europe and Latin America and the Middle East would have to be included to complete the picture."

Clearly, better management of the planet's fresh-water resources is an idea whose time is overdue.

Chapter Five

Two

Case

Studies

Two of the areas included in Sandra Postel's Worldwatch Institute report serve as examples of what happens when a combination of the factors involved in water shortages and competition come together in one place. These two are the Middle East and the American West. Both are experiencing an intense scramble for fresh-water resources.

CALIFORNIA

California has earned the reputation for being on the cutting edge of technology and development, and that is the case where water is concerned. For almost 50 years California has used more surface water than any other state, and has led the nation in groundwater withdrawals. To complicate water management and distribution, the northern half of the state gets the bulk of the rainfall while the southern half has the bulk of the population and, therefore, water consumption.

Southern California includes hundreds of miles of coastline and prime real estate blessed with a mild climate yearlong. It also includes close to half of the state's total population and is still growing. No city in the arid and populous southern half of the state has received more publicity because of water problems than Los Angeles. The greater Los Angeles area could well be the most water hungry desert-turned-urban-sprawl in the world.

In the early 1900s, when Los Angeles had a population of about 100,000 residents, city officials realized the need for

more water to meet the demands of a continuing influx of people. They engineered a 250-mile gravity flow aqueduct to supply water from the Owens River. Then the inevitable happened. The new supply of water, added to the attraction of a mild climate, stimulated both the city's population growth and the agricultural growth of nearby San Fernando Valley. As a result, more water was soon needed. The engineers went back to the Owens River basin, but this time residents and farmers of the valley objected. Both sides were caught up in a controversy that erupted in violent confrontations. Now, after 20 years of court battles, Los Angeles has just agreed to limit its water withdrawal from Owens Valley to allow for the environmental maintenance of the river basin.

Los Angeles looked farther north for water and decided to tap the Mono Lake basin on the eastern side of the Sierra foothills. Another 100 miles of line was added to the aqueduct from the Owens River to deliver water diverted from four creeks that fed into the lake. In a few years the water level of the lake had subsided and the salinity increased to such an extent that the National Audubon Society filed a suit against Los Angeles based on environmental concern. The case resulted in a California Supreme Court decision that the beneficial use of Mono Lake water by Los Angeles must balance with the public trust value of keeping the water flowing into that natural resource. Eventually withdrawal from the creeks was severely cut back, although Los Angeles still gets some water from the Mono Lake basin.

Los Angeles continued to grow and inevitably turned to the Colorado River for what officials saw as a reliable and adequate water supply to keep up with the never-ending demand. Seven times, the seven Colorado basin states—Ari-

zona, California, Colorado, Nevada, New Mexico, Utah, and Wyoming—met in 1921 as members of the Colorado River Commission to resolve the dispute over water rights and allocation. Seven times they failed. Even after six of the seven states ratified the Colorado River Compact, Arizona stood in the way of Southern California's desperate need for both water and flood control. It was not until 1928 that the issue was partially resolved and the building of the Hoover Dam was approved. Eventually, the Parker Dam, built downstream from the larger Hoover Dam, provided a reservoir to supply water to Southern California via the Colorado River Aqueduct.

The Metropolitan Water District of Southern California, formed in 1928, was the agency put in charge of building the aqueduct to supply water from the Colorado for Los Angeles and the mushrooming communities of the southern half of the state. By 1941, the 242-mile-long, $220 million Colorado River Aqueduct was ready, just in time to stimulate an even greater population explosion. Within a few years, the Metropolitan was servicing an area as far south as San Diego and as far east as Pasadena, supplying four million people with water.

Today, the Metropolitan Water District serves almost 15 million people living in 6 counties covering 5,200 square miles of the state with a population increase of 350,000 people a year. That is like adding a city the size of Boston every 12 months. The district is so extensive that if it were a nation, it would rank 12th in the world in gross national product.

California's agricultural need for water grew along with its population. To provide federally subsidized water for the state's agricultural interests, the Bureau of Reclamation engi-

neered the Central Valley Project, which developed water resources from the Sacramento and San Joaquin rivers. When still more water was needed, the State Water Project was developed to supply both agricultural and urban demands. Today it maintains a massive complex of facilities, dams, reservoirs, canals, and aqueducts in an effort to manage statewide water problems and to help satisfy the thirsty southern end of the state.

The Southern California city of Santa Barbara, about 100 miles north of Los Angeles, is one of the few major municipalities that until very recently refused to hook into the State Water Project. Santa Barbara held out because both residents and officials were afraid that state water would artificially stimulate growth and because of local policies for self-sufficiency in natural resources. Besides, officials believed that local water resources were adequate for the growth that was expected. By the mid-1980s this proved to be wrong. Officials studied several possible solutions, each of them thwarted by local water rights or environmental issues. In 1990 the severe drought affecting the local area forced radical rationing on the city. City residents were forbidden to water their lawns and had to restrict other uses or pay very high prices for water. City demand was cut 45 percent in the first year of the emergency.

After paying into the State Water Project all those years without using it, voters approved connecting with the State Water Project in 1991 as one means of solving their crippling water shortage. Residents also voted to build a desalination plant to ensure their future water supply. Soon after the city's long-term water shortage was solved, the rains came, an 18-inch monsoon in the month of February 1992, filling the nearby Cachuma Reservoir with a three-year sup-

Get water wise. Go to the library and ask to see a copy of the U.S. Geological Survey. This will give you information about how much water your state has compared with other states, and how much your state uses in comparison to the rest of the country.

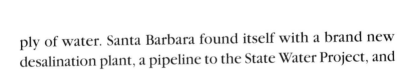

ply of water. Santa Barbara found itself with a brand new desalination plant, a pipeline to the State Water Project, and a reservoir about to spill over.

Before it finally rained hard enough that winter of 1991–1992 to make a difference, two critical things happened in California. First, a six-and-a-half year drought caused severe water shortages throughout the state, reviving the long-standing competition between northern and southern residents. Second, Arizona was ready to claim its rights to a big share of the Colorado River water granted for the state's Central Arizona Project by a 1964 Supreme Court decision. This would cut in half the Metropolitan Water District's allotment of its Colorado River diversion.

These two factors triggered a third major milestone in the state's water shortage, a warning by the State Water Resources Control Board that drastic across-the-board cutbacks appeared necessary. Just when the summer demand for water was peaking, the Metropolitan Water District's supply from the State Water Project was cut by 31 percent. Some local agencies immediately put into effect an even higher mandatory reduction in water use. It looked as if cutbacks would deliver a near fatal blow to California's important agricultural industry. The four biggest agricultural water uses in the state are for cotton, rice, and alfalfa production, and irrigating pastureland for livestock. Each of them relies on subsidized water for irrigation.

The public began to ask why state officials waited so long to call for cutbacks and conservation. Shouldn't something have been done before the water situation was so critical that it threatened not only agriculture but the state's entire economy? They pointed to the fact that California's water shortage did not happen in a day or even in a year. The reservoirs were visibly low and getting lower for several years. Actually, the state's water resources were being closely monitored. Cutbacks in allocation were being made all along, following a formula based on how much rainfall and snow the state received in a given year and the condition of lakes, rivers, and aquifers.

Fortunately, at the last moment California got a partial reprieve when the first of a series of winter storms hit the state. It rained long and hard enough to make a temporary difference, although not enough to fill all the reservoirs nor reverse serious drought conditions. Arizona and five other states that draw on the Colorado agreed to help by letting California have its full share of the river's water for at least

another year. Even so, the potential social and economic impact of the 1991 water crisis will not be quickly forgotten.

Since no one knew if California's reprieve was going to be short-lived, every water agency in the state was searching for new resources and for ways to stretch the existing supply. It looked as if the public's popular "California life-style" based on the myth of water's inexhaustibility was going to have to be changed in favor of "BMP," best management practices. Conservation measures were followed and enforced more extensively. Wastewater reclamation facilities were being built and expanded throughout the state. Desalination was one of the long-term solutions seriously studied in the coastal area. The Metropolitan Water District got busy on plans to put in at least one additional desalination plant, and to construct an 800,000 acre-foot reservoir in southern California that would enable them to store water for use during times of critical need. The situation looked so bleak that even such a "far out" idea as running a pipeline 1,700 miles along the ocean bed from Alaska to California at a cost of $100 billion was seriously considered and promoted by a few officials in high places. Meanwhile the city of Los Angeles continued its pattern of growth with no end in sight.

Then the real rains came. Up and down the state, it rained until every reservoir was full and everyone and everything was waterlogged. The city of Los Angeles itself got 27 inches during the season, which put it 170 percent above normal. Even so, the Metropolitan Water District's plans for desalination, reclamation, and conservation have not changed. All their projects are still on line. They don't ever want to be caught high-and-dry again. The southern half of California is desert country, and its pattern of long droughts

broken by a single winter of heavy rainfall will no doubt continue to be repeated.

THE MIDDLE EAST

Mark Twain's witty comment, "Whiskey is for drinkin', water is for fightin'," suits the situation in the Mideast, where fresh-water resources are replacing oil as the probable cause for the next international war. While Egypt, Ethiopia, Sudan, and Uganda are staking out claims in the Nile River basin, and Iraq, Syria, and Turkey eye one another over the Tigris-Euphrates river system, Lebanon, Jordan, and Syria are competing with Israel over water rights.

The same factors involved in Los Angeles are responsible for the militant competition for fresh-water resources in the Mideast. Populations continue to increase, bringing with them an increase in industry and agriculture and a need for more water. Problems of supply and demand are made worse by poor or nonexistent management. International funds have helped pay for Mideast water projects in the past, but because of political and economic complications, many of the problems have not been solved. Some facilities are badly in need of improvements, are not operated at capacity, or are run inefficiently, resulting in much waste.

One factor not found in Los Angeles is the political and religious hostility that keeps countries from working together. There is little cooperation among Mideast nations, except for occasional talks. Sometimes even the talks are lacking. In this atmosphere of tense distrust, high-level negotiations on water issues have not come about. Yet, here as elsewhere, economic survival is tied to water. If war is to be avoided, a solution must be found soon.

Contact your local County Water
Authority and see about organizing
a Water Awareness Month.
They know all of the other city, county,
state, and federal water agencies you
can call to take part. They will also visit
your school to show educational films
and videos, conduct programs, and
sponsor poster contests.

Not only has Israel's population increased dramatically,
but its national average use of water per person per day is at
least five times as much as in neighboring countries. Israel
at present is using 95 percent of its available water
resources. By the year 2000, it will be short by one-third
of its needs. Meanwhile, one million Soviet Jews are waiting to be resettled within that troubled country's borders
or in areas considered by many to be outside Israel's legal
borders.

Since 1948 Israel has multiplied sixfold the acres depen-

dent on irrigation for cultivation. Although Israeli farmers are admittedly among the most water-efficient in the world, the government may soon have to choose between water-intensive crops, such as cotton, and critical domestic and industrial needs. The continued irrigation of acres of cotton fields is contributing to the serious overuse of regional groundwater resources and their contamination by pesticide and fertilizer runoff and salinization. For these reasons irrigation also contributes to the unfriendly relations between Israel and its neighbors.

Israel's main water sources are the Sea of Galilee, the Jordan River, and several major aquifers, but none of these are without problems. In recent years the Sea of Galilee has been greatly depleted to provide for a wide range of development projects. The Jordan serves as a water supply upstream of the Sea of Galilee but not downstream, where it is too contaminated with salt to be useful. And the aquifers are only partly located within Israel's borders. Most of the groundwater withdrawal comes from a reservoir beneath the occupied territories of the West Bank and Gaza Strip, and from a series of seashore aquifers along the Mediterranean Sea.

The water situation in the Gaza Strip is said to be a time bomb waiting to explode. Israel's presence there and its use of that water resource are hotly contested by Palestinians and on their behalf by Lebanon, Syria, and Jordan. To make matters worse, salt-water intrusion caused by Israel's overpumping threatens to contaminate that aquifer, making it useless as far as everyone's needs are concerned.

The most water-rich nation in that area of the world is Turkey, whose President Özal has been campaigning for a project known as the "peace pipeline." The proposal was

first made several years ago when Turkish officials offered to build a pipeline to supply water from their ample resources to nations with chronic shortages. The supply line would be the longest water-delivery system in the world, stretching 3,730 miles from Turkey south to the Arabian Peninsula, east to Kuwait, and west to Lebanon and Israel.

So far, none of the other Mideast nations has been enthusiastic about Turkey's proposal. First, it would cost $20 billion, a sum not easy to come by even if international funding were available. Second, the countries that would benefit most from the pipeline, Israel and Syria, are not anxious to become dependent on Turkey for anything as vital as water. They question what they would be forced to do if for some reason Turkey decided to shut off the supply.

Turkish officials assure everyone that this will not happen. They insist that the peace pipeline is a genuine effort by them to ease the region's tensions over water, not create new ones. Officials do not deny that Turkey stands to make money on the project, but they point out that it would also save money for those countries who would be paying about half of what desalination plants will cost.

In spite of not wanting to be put in a position of dependency, Israel is trying to negotiate with Turkey for water it desperately needs. Turkey recently completed construction of the giant Ataturk Dam as part of its Southeast Anatolia Project and intends to build 21 other dams to irrigate 46,000 acres of semiarid land of its own. This massive development of hydroelectrical dams and irrigation systems uses water from the upper Tigris and Euphrates rivers. It is part of Turkey's hope to become the grain, fruit, and vegetable market for all the Mideast and to generate enough electrical power to sell.

Last year when Turkey diverted 75 percent of the flow of the Euphrates for about a month to start filling the Ataturk Dam, other Euphrates users were in an uproar. Syria and Iraq, usually rivals, formed a pact against Turkey to protest its position as the water superpower of the region. The Southeast Anatolia Project could eventually cut Syria's water supply almost in half and be just one more reason for hard feelings. National tempers have cooled somewhat, but the situation is too tense for international comfort.

Iraq is last in line for water from the Tigris and Euphrates rivers, so her supply of water will be drastically cut by Turkey's upstream Southeast Anatolia Project, possibly by as much as two-thirds. Apart from an agreement signed by Turkey and Syria in 1987 giving Syria a set amount of Euphrates water, there is no formal international agreement among Turkey, Iraq, and Syria on the sharing of water from the Tigris-Euphrates systems, nor among Jordan, Syria, and Israel on use of the Jordan River. Both situations are on hold for the time being.

Because of their mutual dependence in the Yarmuk River, Syria and Jordan have come to an agreement on construction of the Unity Dam on that waterway. Jordan uses the Yarmuk to irrigate the fertile Jordan Valley. Israel also uses some water from the Yarmuk to supplement her supply from the Sea of Galilee. Meanwhile Syria eventually wants to build a series of smaller dams to divert 40 percent of the Yarmuk her way. With the prospect of a reduced flow from the Euphrates, and the threat of even more severe contamination and salinization of the region's water resources, Syria is planning ahead just in case the terms of her agreement with Jordan are not kept.

Ten years of drought in the Mideast, of excessive with-

Find out about your state's major waterways and aquifers and how they are used. Find out if they are used to supply the needs of any industries and, if so, what happens to the wastewater from these industries.

drawals, and of international distrust have taken their toll on water resources and on national tempers. Last year's rainy season was the driest in 70 years. Saudi Arabia's deep drill wells, which cost untold amounts of money, have lowered the water table by seven to eight feet. A recent report based on work done by the United States Geological Survey concluded that almost all of Saudi Arabia's groundwater comes from nonrenewable fossil water aquifers that could run out in the near future. Although some officials in Saudi Arabia do not acknowledge the "nonrenewability" of their resources, nevertheless the lowering of the water table is cause for concern.

Libya is also drawing on fossil water resources to irrigate expanded wheat fields and provide for livestock. The cost

of depleting these nonrenewable resources cannot be measured solely in dollars, but in what it would do to the future of the nation and to the region as a whole. Before that happens, global water experts suggest that there be an immediate and serious effort to make sure that every drop of the fossil water being withdrawn is put to the best possible use.

Since there are no surface water resources within its borders, Libya has been working on a massive project of its own for the past seven years, building a great man-made river with water pumped from under the Sahara Desert. The cost is expected to be $25 billion, even more than Turkey's peace pipeline. As of now, only the first phase of the 1,200 mile, 13-foot diameter pipeline has been completed, delivering 500,000 gallons of water a day for irrigation and urban use. Four more phases are planned, which could make this man-made river the largest civil engineering project in the world.

Lebanon has enough surface and groundwater resources, and the rainfall to recharge them, to meet her needs and become a regional "water broker" along with Turkey. Instead the country is struggling with a severe freshwater shortage. The capital city of Beirut is especially hard hit. Lebanon's coastal aquifers are damaged by seawater intrusion, its farmlands are without adequate water for irrigation, and civil war has left its pipelines in need of major repair. These problems stem from many factors, including a chronic lack of proper management and development of national resources. They not only hamper Lebanon's wellbeing, but they put the country at odds with its neighbors in the competition for water.

All of these national issues, and the suspicions they

arouse among Mideast countries, aggravate the region's unstable water situation.

The international community is helping to look for solutions before competition gets any more critical. The World Bank and other similar lending agencies are deeply interested and involved. So is the United States, and through USAID has offered technical assistance and sponsored scientific exchanges, workshops, and feasibility studies. A number of government agencies and organizations have extended their activities to work with foreign water officials in any way they can.

Solar energy is being considered to power desalination plants in the region, cutting the cost of operation by as much as half. There is hope that **hydrogeologists** will begin mapping the area to pinpoint water-bearing **strata** where new groundwater resources may be located, such as the recent important sites discovered in Egypt. One of the latest methods of finding such underground reservoirs is through satellite remote sensing studies now being carried on in Oman, at the southeast tip of the Saudi Arabian peninsula. If this exploratory information were available, it would be a significant basis for the peaceful resolution of the region's water problems.

Another promising possibility is growing **halophytes**, which are salt-tolerant crops, to use as livestock feed to conserve limited fresh-water resources. Halophytes survive on saline water irrigation, making them practical for the coastal area of the Mediterranean Sea, Persian Gulf, and Red Sea, where brackish (salty) groundwater is common.

Most of all, a search is on for ways to get high-level negotiations started before the prediction of a Mideast water war becomes a reality.

Chapter Six

Looking

to the

Future

DOES FRESH WATER HAVE A FUTURE? HAS THE HUMAN POPULATION'S use and abuse of water resources put planet earth in jeopardy?

If the Earth Summit held in Rio de Janiero in June 1992 is any indication, people may finally be ready to act responsibly. During that Summit, the world looked at itself and its relation to natural resources. The discussions were sometimes political, but they opened the door to exciting possibilities.

The basis for the Earth Summit is Agenda 21, framed ten years ago by the United Nations. It is being called "the new Magna Carta," and resolves to do something about global environmental concerns including water resources. Several chapters of Agenda 21 are on water-related subjects, but chapter 18 is specifically on "Water, its protection and management." Here is how it reads:

> Fresh water, once a free good like air, is rapidly becoming a commodity like petroleum. The human population, especially in its urban conglomerations and on the marginal lands now brought under cultivation, confronts water as the limiting element in its existence. Water is the earliest necessity required by human metabolism from hour to hour, and it is the contamination of water that sickens most of the sick. Agenda 21 here sets out measures, from development of long-range weather and climate forecasting to cleanup of the most obvious sources of pollution, to secure the supply of fresh water for the next doubling of the human population.

The estimated cost for implementing these measures is $54.7 billion, including $17 billion for technical and economic assistance. But the cost of doing nothing is even greater.

Most of the experts who took part in the Rio de Janiero conference agree that the water situation is bad but not hopeless. There is still time to act, to treat fresh water with the respect it deserves as uniquely important to individual and global well-being. The technology exists and solutions are at hand to reverse the results of years of careless use both in the United States and the rest of the world.

The solutions being considered are as varied as the water problems themselves. They focus mainly on such means as conservation, reclamation, better management of resources, pollution control, desalination, and public education. They involve federal and state agencies, the water users, public groups and organizations, and concerned citizens.

If a penny saved is a penny earned, then a gallon of water saved is a gallon added to the public supply. Conserving water can be as simple as not letting the water run while brushing your teeth or as complicated as maintaining the total circulatory system in operation at Hamilton Lake in Itasca, Illinois, where state-of-the-art engineering includes the use of reclaimed water to maintain a self-sufficient project for that entire development. Every major water user is involved in some form of water conservation.

Farmers are in a position to save millions of gallons of fresh water by replacing overhead sprinklers with efficient drip irrigation systems or low-energy precision application systems. Both methods water crops closer to the ground, cutting back on wasteful over-watering and evaporation.

The key to successful conservation is to use the most appropriate watering system for each specific crop.

Agriculture can do more **rain fed farming**, which involves seasonal planting and eliminates the need to irrigate. Farmers can and are cutting back on beef production, which requires acres of irrigated pastureland, and are finding substitutes for water-intensive crops such as alfalfa, cotton, and rice. The federal government has the means to help by funding international agricultural research centers where new strains of drought-resistant and salt-tolerant crops can be developed.

Surprising as it may seem, agricultural conservation is influenced by the eating habits of the general public. We are no longer a meat-and-potatoes nation. Health-food stores and organic-produce markets are springing up in most neighborhoods. Soy products have long been used by vegetarian groups, but now they are being offered by grocery stores and fast food outlets. The amount of water needed to produce a pound of beef can produce many more pounds of soy-derived nutrition.

Agricultural research may soon provide farmers with another way to conserve by cleaning up feedlot and packing plant lagoons using a biological process that removes the stench and the pollutants from what is normally wastewater. The process is so economically attractive that it has been patented by Ian Rosebrook, an environmental engineer who came up with the idea. His solution uses a mix of all-natural "bugs" or decay-eating organisms to reduce the nitrate level in some cases to zero, producing lots of oxygen at the same time. As a result the water is clean and aerated enough for frogs and fish to live in. It can be pumped back into creek beds or reused for irrigation. Use of this type of

bio-remediation to treat all kinds of wastewater is one of the most promising solutions of the future.

A cooperative conservation plan in effect in Southern California involves the Metropolitan Water District (MWD) financing the improvement and upgrading of the Imperial Irrigation District's faulty distribution system to cut back on irrigation water lost in transit. According to one estimate, as much as 50 percent of our national water supply and 75 percent of Europe's water supply is lost through poorly designed distribution systems, leaks, and evaporation, so a coaction plan like this is a major solution. The MWD gets the millions of gallons of water saved, which in turn will save them an estimated $710 million over 20 years. Best of all, the conservation plan is a cost-effective way to help meet Southern California's need for more water without tapping new resources.

Since most household water goes for showers, flush toilets, and lawn and garden sprinklers, a significant number of gallons will be saved per family per day as updated state plumbing codes go into effect. Some cities require that low-flow shower heads and toilets as water-economical as 1.6 gallons a flush be installed in all new buildings. Retrofit rebates help defray the cost of replacing old plumbing fixtures. Leak detection and repair programs cut back on thousands of gallons that literally go down the drain. Water-saving drip systems and drought-resistant plants are required for landscaping new commercial and housing development projects in arid regions. Savings of up to 70 percent of water use are expected this way.

Industries from coast to coast are involved in water volume cutback programs. Even though the East Coast is not experiencing the intense shortage and competition felt in

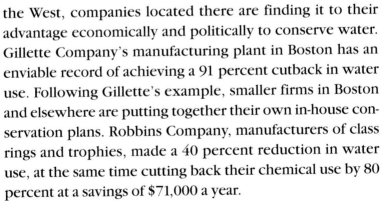

Write to your Congresspeople and Representatives, asking what they are doing to protect the water in your state. Their names and addresses should be listed in the phone book, or you can easily find out who they are at the library.

the West, companies located there are finding it to their advantage economically and politically to conserve water. Gillette Company's manufacturing plant in Boston has an enviable record of achieving a 91 percent cutback in water use. Following Gillette's example, smaller firms in Boston and elsewhere are putting together their own in-house conservation plans. Robbins Company, manufacturers of class rings and trophies, made a 40 percent reduction in water use, at the same time cutting back their chemical use by 80 percent at a savings of $71,000 a year.

Probably one of the most exciting and practical solutions of the future is the use of reclaimed water to supplement fresh-water resources. In 1991 the Symposium on Water

Supply and Reuse sponsored by the American Water Resources Association in San Diego, California, brought together thousands of technicians, engineers, environmental planners, district managers, hydrologists, project directors, and just plain people to talk about reclamation.

The idea is not new, but shortages and competition for fresh-water resources have made the use of a readily available and dependable supply of wastewater extremely practical. Reclaimed water is the only growing water resource on tap for water planners. Besides, advanced methods of treatment can now completely restore such water to drinkable quality.

The idea of using reclaimed water as a potable supply has never been generally acceptable to the American public, nevertheless research to that end is being done in Colorado, California, and Florida. The Potable Water Reuse Demonstration Plant in Colorado has been producing high quality water for the public water system since 1984. In South Africa, potable reuse is being evaluated at facilities in Pretoria, Cape Town, Cape Flats, and Namibia. The city of Windhoek, Namibia, already has a full-scale direct potable reclamation system that started operating in 1969. It originally provided about one-third of the city's water supply and is still in use today when fresh water supplies run low. It includes the most advanced technical processes and is a good working model for scientific studies.

While potable reuse has been frowned on in the United States, many cities found other acceptable uses for reclaimed water. As early as 1965, a dual system was installed in Grand Canyon National Park with two separate lines, one for fresh water and one for reclaimed water used for outdoor landscape, cooling, and toilet flushing. The city of

Lubbock, Texas, developed its highly successful Canyon Lakes Project using excess wastewater from nearby agricultural farms. Now, thirty years later, this Texas-size oasis continues to be a popular haven for fishing and family recreation. In Denver, Colorado, limited water supplies do not meet the needs of the New Denver International Airport, so reclaimed water will provide for nonpotable uses.

El Paso, Texas, has a prototype **direct injection** project, meaning reclaimed wastewater is introduced directly into a fresh-water resource thereby serving as a groundwater recharge. The El Paso project pumps highly treated water into ten deep wells from where it eventually finds its way into the city's potable water system. Another direct injection system is used in the Occoquan Reservoir in Virginia to supply as much as 80 to 90 percent of the reservoir's inflow during droughts. In Clayton County, Georgia, reclaimed water provides irrigation for forests in the reservoir's watershed, recharging the groundwater resource and raising the water table.

The treatment of wastewater has come a long way since the early days when European-style croplands irrigated with effluent (waste material) from treatment plants were labeled as "sewage farms." Today, reclaimed water is no longer physically offensive, and in fact is admittedly more practical than fresh water because it contains nutrients needed for healthy growth and soil enrichment. With shortages becoming more widespread, federal subsidies being phased out, and the cost of water expected to go up, agriculture has every reason to find reclamation attractive.

Suburban districts burdened with great amounts of wastewater are being encouraged to find ways to get the

reclaimed water to the farmer at a reasonable cost. City officials are planning on a dramatic increase in agricultural reuse. This is happening in many states where competing fresh-water users have no place else to look for a future supply but to cutbacks in irrigation.

Reclamation is a proven way to restore wetlands, create new ones, and maintain those in danger of being lost. Using reclaimed water fits in with the recent recommendation by the National Academy of Sciences for Congress to establish a long-term wetlands recovery strategy. Even though administration officials in Washington have not taken the lead on the issue of wetlands restoration, some communities are going ahead on their own. The townspeople in Arcata, California, fought a long and complicated battle to re-create a natural filtration system of marshes and ponds rather than spending millions on a much needed wastewater treatment plant. What was once an unsightly landfill known as "Mount Trashmore" is now 150 acres of reclaimed wetlands teeming with wildlife and people who visit Arcata to learn how to use reclamation to save money and a wetlands at the same time.

The state of Louisiana, one of the leading states in wetlands losses, is another example of what people can do on their own initiative. Voters there passed a landmark referendum to set aside a portion of oil and gas severance taxes to pay for restoration of their remaining wetlands.

Industry is turning to at least partial use of reclaimed water for cooling towers, following the successful record of the Bethlehem Steel plant at Sparrows Point in Baltimore, Maryland, in operation since 1942. The Chevron USA refinery in Richmond, California, expects to complete its new reclamation facility for cooling tower use in 1993, the largest industrial reuse project in the state.

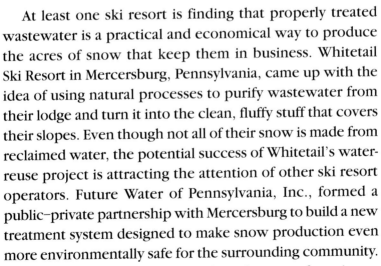

Find out what the United States is doing to help conserve water worldwide. Write to the president and encourage him to participate in any upcoming Earth Summits.

At least one ski resort is finding that properly treated wastewater is a practical and economical way to produce the acres of snow that keep them in business. Whitetail Ski Resort in Mercersburg, Pennsylvania, came up with the idea of using natural processes to purify wastewater from their lodge and turn it into the clean, fluffy stuff that covers their slopes. Even though not all of their snow is made from reclaimed water, the potential success of Whitetail's water-reuse project is attracting the attention of other ski resort operators. Future Water of Pennsylvania, Inc., formed a public–private partnership with Mercersburg to build a new treatment system designed to make snow production even more environmentally safe for the surrounding community.

The biggest hurdle that stands in the way of maximum

use of reclaimed water is the NIMBY syndrome, the attitude of "not in my back yard," accepting reclamation only as long as it is somewhere else. Studies of public attitudes show a definite pattern both for and against reuse of treated wastewater. As a general rule, men are more tolerant toward the idea than women, the younger, affluent groups more than older, poorer people. All indications, however, point to greater overall acceptance as technology eliminates negative factors regarding health risks or aesthetics.

One of the first steps toward a solution to shortages and competition is a national agreement on the economics of water, no longer treating it as a commodity without price or value. If major water users are encouraged to "kick the cheap water habit," then management can use every means at hand to make better use of fresh-water resources.

The economics of water is one reason eastern states are opposed to continuing federal subsidies for western and southwestern expansion. Subsidies were more or less accepted as necessary in the 1920s and 1930s, but now they are looked on as an unfair advantage that is limiting eastern economic development. The East does not want to give up its water-rich status unless the price is right and unless its local needs are protected before an expected flow westward begins.

This same strategy is partly responsible for bringing about the Great Lakes Charter signed in 1985 by governors of eight Great Lakes states and two Canadian premiers. Its purpose is the regional management of any and all withdrawals from that body of water, keeping the West or any other outsider from taking economic advantage. The charter signatories are wary of the possibility that some federal agency will decide to export their water. One Great Lakes

official is quoted as objecting, "If you export water, you export jobs."

Whether the concept of the charter is legal will have to be tested in court. Water laws in the United States require that the resources of a community be used for the benefit of all. The question is, does the term "all" exclude or include beneficial needs outside the Great Lakes region?

The economics of water management is behind the idea of water banks recently established in several states as a means of resources management. The Idaho Snake River water bank functions like a market for water exchanges. Water can be "rented" for any beneficial use such as irrigation, and paid for after the irrigation season. Banks are particularly useful during droughts when they solve problems of supply and demand.

In 1991, as a means of better management, California started its own water bank, allowing farmers to sell some of the water allotted to them through the State Water Project for other needs within the state.

Through charters and water banks, and through the many national and international symposiums, conferences, task forces, water courts, and foundations that are looking for solutions to water problems, management is finding the tools to do what it needs to do to make the most of global water resources.

Of all the major water users in the United States, industry probably has made the greatest progress toward finding a solution to pollution. Many large companies have found that it is cheaper to produce less waste than to dispose of greater amounts safely. Massachusetts, one of the major waste-exporting states, passed a Toxics Use Reduction Act, setting a goal of decreasing industrial toxic chemical waste by 50

percent by 1997. While state initiatives such as this, combined with action by the EPA as the federal law enforcement agency, are pushing for pollution control, industry itself has taken the lead on in-house programs to minimize the amount of waste produced.

Waste reduction has been a part of the global Du Pont Company since 1982 when it joined the Chemical Manufacturers Association, whose aim is "to develop and produce chemicals that can be manufactured, transported, used, and disposed of safely." By 1990 Du Pont had achieved a 35 percent cutback on waste, saving tens of millions of dollars in the process. The company's goal is to reach a 60 percent reduction by 1993 and 90 percent by the year 2000.

Since 1975 Minnesota Mining and Manufacturing Company, better known as 3M, has been a leader with their 3P program, meaning "pollution prevention pays." Dow Chemical Company has a similar program it calls WRAP for "waste reduction always pays." As a matter of fact, pollution reduction does not always pay. In some instances and for some processes, cleaning up after the pollution has been created is the only way smaller companies can afford to stay in business. But as environmental cleanup costs rise, pollution prevention is becoming a practical priority.

Other companies cutting back on pollution include the Polaroid Corporation, which expects to reach its goal of 50 percent reduction in both toxic chemical use and waste by 1993. Digital Equipment Corporation has reduced use of chlorofluorocarbon solvents to clean circuit boards by developing a new aqueous solution. Glidden Company changed the formula for all the paint they manufacture except flat latex to meet standards set by the Clean Air law. Procter and Gamble packages 80 percent of its products in

Keep up with water in the news. Look for articles about water and other conservation issues in the newspapers and magazines. Watch the nightly news to learn about environmental issues in your area and worldwide.

recycled paper, is introducing refillable containers, and is experimenting with a process to make plant food and other useful products from disposable diapers. "Mc Recycle USA" is McDonald Corporation's program to use biodegradable carry-out bags made of recycled newspaper. This popular fast-food chain is also spending $100 million a year to use recycled material in their building projects.

Research teams in many states are coming up with important new ideas to reduce pollution. Marine biologists at New Mexico State University's Roswell Test Facility are working with the Department of Energy on a pilot-scale experiment to grow salt-water algae that holds promise of providing an alternate source of hydrocarbon fuel. The algae contains **lipids** biologists hope to extract and convert

into gasoline and fuel similar to diesel at a cost comparable with today's price at the pumps. Since New Mexico has 15 billion acre-feet of saline groundwater that up to now has been useless, the project is doubly important.

Tejas Resources, Inc.'s new battery recycling plant at Terrell, Texas, will be the world's first totally enclosed lead-acid recycling facility. Groundwater pollution from improperly buried or dumped automotive batteries is a problem of national and international concern.

A new plastic resin made almost entirely from starch has been developed by Warner-Lambert Company, known for its health-care products. Called Novon, the bio-plastic starch is completely degradable and is being hailed as a spectacular breakthrough in replacing petroleum-based plastic. The new resin is made from starch extracted from wheat and such vegetables as corn, rice, and potatoes. And researchers at Michigan State University in East Lansing and James Madison University in Harrisonburg, Virginia, have biogenetically engineered a plant that will produce degradable plastic and do so economically.

Besides the advantage of producing environmentally friendly plastics, researchers are discovering better ways to recycle them. Some experts predict that up to 30 percent of all plastics produced worldwide could be recycled. Firms like BMW, General Motors, and Ford are working on how to increase the recycling of plastics now being used in automobile manufacture. BMW has a test program in the United States that offers a $500 rebate for turning in an old BMW for recycling when buying a new one.

These examples are but a few of the solution-to-pollution ideas expected to make a difference in the near future.

When it comes to solving the problem of pollution from

garbage disposal, Ontario, Canada, has an idea that is as literally "far out" as the Alaska/California pipeline. This city of more than three million residents has contracted to ship 4,000 tons of garbage a day via specially built railway cars to an abandoned mine 375 miles north. The contract runs for 20 years and will move 30 million tons of trash at a cost of $450 million. The plan includes a recycling plant at the dump site to separate usable materials and a pumping station to keep seepage from contaminating possible groundwater resources.

Opponents to the garbage train plan say it will only encourage Ontario residents to continue their outrageous garbage production habits instead of practicing their "3 Rs" of reduce, reuse, and recycle. Besides, because of weather conditions, when the garbage arrives at the mine site most of the time it will be railcar-size blocks of frozen, unsorted trash. What will this do to the plan to recycle loads before they are dumped? Environmental hearings will soon determine if the garbage train idea is a visionary solution or just a costly postponement of the city's need to bite the waste bullet.

A much more practical idea on what to do about garbage is to excavate landfills and reuse the sites for parkland or other community needs. Collier County, Florida, pioneered a program to recycle wastes buried in landfills and is making it pay off financially. In Lancaster County, Pennsylvania, landfill material is mined to provide fuel for energy plants that burn wastes. The possibility of reclaiming landfill material could go a long way toward solving the need to remove potential environmental threats and make old sites reusable.

Even though desalination of seawater has been in use for many years, it takes so much energy to provide power for

either **thermal distillation** or the **reverse osmosis process** that so far in most cases desalting has not been generally cost-effective, except where there was no alternative.

Reverse osmosis forces seawater through membranes under hydrolic pressure. The saltier the water, the higher pressure membranes needed and the more kilowatt hours it takes to do the job. Two to four gallons of seawater treated this way yield one gallon of fresh water. In the multi-flash process, the most common method of thermal distillation, hot seawater is passed through as many as 40 steam chambers where the heat produces desalted vapor. Using this type of evaporation, it takes ten gallons of seawater for each gallon of fresh water produced.

At present two-thirds of the world's desalinated water is produced on the Arabian Peninsula, where oil-rich countries can afford operation costs. Most of these plants use multi-flash evaporation. Their operation was in jeopardy when Iraq pumped 100,000 barrels of crude oil a day into the Persian Gulf during the recent Mideast conflict. The oil would have put the plants out of commission if it had been sucked up by the intake valves.

Even though there are a great number of desalting plants in the United States, some of them are very small, and the national percentage of fresh water supplied this way is also small. One of the oldest and largest facilities was put into operation in the United States Virgin Islands in 1964 when the population began to outgrow the available resources. Even now desalination is hard pressed to keep ahead of population there. In Florida, because of the poor quality and uneven distribution of fresh water, about 100 desalination facilities are used to supplement the state's abundant resources. All of Florida's plants treat

saline groundwater rather than seawater.

In spite of cost, desalting is one of the future solutions being expanded in Southern California. In addition to the new facility in Santa Barbara, three new projects are being studied: the Baja Desalination Project near the Mexican border, a Metropolitan Water District demonstration plant along the southern coastal area, and a project in which the San Diego Gas and Electric Company would repower its South Bay facility and build a reverse osmosis plant in cooperation with the San Diego County Water Authority.

Through education a change is slowly coming about in people's attitudes toward fresh water. It is no longer socially acceptable to take it for granted. Shortages and other water issues are in the news almost every day. Even in regions where fresh water is abundant, the message is coming across that demand is catching up with supply. Nothing short of public education can prevent future global crises.

Without question, one of the most effective organizations dedicated to public education on the subject of water is the League of Women Voters. Not only have they carried out an extensive State and Community Water Quality Issues Survey, but they published the findings, making them available to state and federal officials. One of the league's four key goals is to broaden public understanding of all the current issues concerning fresh water.

While the League of Women Voters is educating the general public, other groups are working to make young people aware of fresh water as an endangered resource. Many schools have natural science and ecology courses on the subject. Some local and state agencies have officials who visit classrooms and give talks on water resources, conservation, and hydrology.

One of the best such programs is in Nebraska, where a very successful Children's Groundwater Festival is held. At last year's annual festival, 3,000 students were chosen from 7,000 applicants wanting to attend. Fast-paced activities start at 8:30 A.M. and continue until 4:00 P.M. Students and their teachers are bused in from all over Nebraska to take part in more than 65 events ranging from computer games to water magic, from puppet shows to scientific experiments. Some schools have already signed up a year ahead of time to make sure they don't miss out. Susan Seacrest, president of the Nebraska Groundwater Foundation, which sponsors the event, hopes that the festival will go national and possibly international in the near future. Mexico City has already indicated an interest in having a festival of their own.

Many water agencies publish water resources material for elementary and secondary students. Most of it is low cost or free for the asking. The American Water Works Association, the oldest utility group in the United States, has a catalog listing the activity books they publish. The Water Education Foundation located in California and Colorado is another reliable source for information. The Soil and Water Conservation Society puts out a free brochure about their young-reader material that can be ordered by calling 1-800-THE-SOIL.

The American Groundwater Trust offers a full range of posters, videos, comic books, newspapers, coloring books, games, lesson plans, and computer software. Friends of the Earth publishes a guide listing educational material and encourages student clubs such as Kids Against Pollution with chapters in 50 states and several foreign countries. The San Diego County Water Authority uses a character

known as the "Common Waterhog" on billboards and bumper stickers, and in their school programs featuring a live-action movie. The California Department of Water Resources offers a long list of water-awareness material for all age levels.

At Tufts University's Environmental Literacy Institute in Medford, Massachusetts, a roomful of college professors is experiencing an acute social awakening that is shattering the myth that fresh water is an inexhaustible resource. They are asking the question, "What can I do about water?" To find answers, they are learning their environmental three R's. When they have finished the course, they will share their ecological concern with the students they teach and the people they meet and associate with. Now that you have finished reading this book, you are on an environmental par with those professors.

CHRONOLOGY OF MAJOR FEDERAL ACTS CONCERNING WATER

1965–Solid Waste Disposal Act.

1968–National Water Commission created by Congress to review resources problems.

1969–Secretary of the Interior invokes a new Water Quality Act to stop massive discharge of chemicals and sewage waste into streams and lakes.

1970–Earth Day, April 22, declared by Congress to reclaim purity of air, water, and living environment. The motto: "Give earth a chance."

1971–EPA given responsibility for water quality and sets standards for 22 contaminants.

1972–Federal Water Pollution Control Act, called the Clean Water Act, sets "fishable-swimmable" goal to be reached by 1993 and the zero pollutants discharge goal to be reached by 1995.

1973–National Water Commission created to review national water resources problems.

1974–Safe Drinking Water Act. Congress gives the EPA authority in three vital areas: to set drinking water standards; to monitor water quality; and to order the installation of treatment plants. The primary power of enforcement is left with the states.

1976–Resources Conservation and Recovery Act authorizes hazardous waste management.

1977–Clean Water Act reauthorized. First statutary mention of wetlands and their protection.

1980–Comprehensive Environmental Response, Compensation, and Liability Act, known as Superfund, established to clean up leaks from hazardous dumps and spills.

1984–Hazardous and Solid Waste Amendments extended the RCCA to control hazardous waste from "cradle to grave": from generation through transportation, treatment, and disposal.

1986–Safe Drinking Water Act Amendments closed loopholes and called for research; require EPA to review and possibly revise existing drinking water standards; to set primary standards for 9 contaminants within a year, adding 40 more within 2 years, and setting standards for a total of 83 contaminants within 3 years.

1986–Water Resources Development Act authorizes water construction projects and cost sharing provisions.

1986–Superfund Amendments and Reauthorization Act extends its regulations through 1994, with funding at an $8.5 billion level, five times the original amount.

1987–Water Quality Act further amends Clean Water Act. It is the principal law dealing with pollution of streams, lakes, and estuaries.

1987—EPA sets final enforceable primary standards called MCLs (maximum contaminant level) for 8 volatile organic chemicals bringing their total to 30. An additional 13 unenforceable secondary standards are recommended (RMCLs).

1988—Federal Insecticide, Fungicide and Rodentcide Act; "lite" amendments regulate manufacture, use, and disposal of pesticides.

1989—Wetlands Conservation Act backs "no net loss of wetlands" promise.

1990—Clean Air Act Amendments address ambient air quality standards and set new limits on pollution levels regarding ozone depletion, tailpipe emissions, acid rain, and release of air toxins; includes new enforcement procedures and permit requirements; contains a substantive alternative fuel program for private vehicles in California, and for fleet vehicles.

1990—Office of Environmental Quality established.

1990—Waste Reduction Act passed.

1991—Reauthorization of Resources Conservation and Recovery Act and Clean Water Act.

1992—Phase Five rule of the Safe Drinking Water Act sets standards for 24 organic and inorganic compounds effective in 1994.

1992—Federal Facility Compliance Act requires all federal facilities to conform to environmental regulations.

FOR FURTHER READING

Baines, Lucy. *Protecting the Oceans*. Austin, Texas: Steck Vaughn, 1992.

Bender, David, and Bruno Leone, editors. *The Environmental Crisis: Opposing Viewpoints*. San Diego: Greenhaven Press, 1991.

——*Global Resources: Opposing Viewpoints*. San Diego: Greenhaven Press, 1991

Buzzelli, Buzz. *How to Get Water Smart: Products and Practices for Saving Water in the Nineties*. Santa Barbara, Cal.: Terra Firma, 1991.

Gay, Kathlyn. *Water Pollution*. New York: Franklin Watts, 1990.

Hoff, Mary, and Mary M. Rodgers. *Our Endangered Planet: Groundwater*. Minneapolis: Lerner, 1991.

——*Our Endangered Planet: Oceans*. Minneapolis, MN: Lerner, 1991.

O'Neill, Mary. *Water Squeeze*. Mahwah, New Jersey: Troll, 1991.

Slater, William. *Drought Busters: 30 Easy Ways to Save Water—and Money*. Venice, Cal.: Living Planet Press, 1991.

Twist, Clint. S*eas and Oceans*. New York: Dillon Press, 1992.

Von Brook, Patricia, editor. *Water, No Longer Taken for Granted*. Wylie, Texas: Information Plus, 1989.

Woodburn, Judith. *Dying Oceans*. Milwaukee: Gareth Stevens, 1991.

FOR MORE INFORMATION

The groups and organizations listed below can provide you with information on water conservation and other environmental topics.

Center for Marine Conservation
1725 DeSales Street NW
Washington, DC 20036

Citizens for a Better Environment
59 East Van Buren, Suite 1600
Chicago, IL 60605

Clean Water Action Project
733 15th Street NE, Suite 1110
Washington, DC 20005

Environmental Defense Fund
257 Park Avenue South
New York, NY 10010

Environmental Protection Agency
401 M Street SW
Washington, DC 20460

Friends of the Earth
530 7th Street SE
Washington, DC 20009

Greenpeace USA
1436 U Street NW
Washington, DC 20009

Izaak Walton League
1401 Wilson Boulevard, Level B
Arlington, VA 22209

National Oceanic and Atmospheric Administration
U.S. Department of Commerce, Room 5807
Washington, DC 20230

Oceanic Society
1536 16th Street NW
Washington, DC 20036

Student Conservation Association
Box 550
Charlestown, NH 03603

Waste Watch
1346 Connecticut Avenue NW, No. 217
Washington, DC 20036

GLOSSARY

aquifers—Underground reservoirs of water.

artesian well—A well that is formed when water that is under high pressure is forced to the earth's surface.

capillary action—The process by which water travels through the ground either through the roots of plants and trees or between spaces in rocks and layers of earth.

circulation—The various processes by which water is moved through the hydrological cycle.

confined aquifer—Reservoirs that are formed when water is trapped between layers of rock or clay.

direct injection—An experimental process in which reclaimed wastewater is returned directly to fresh-water sources to replenish supplies.

drought—A prolonged period of no precipitation in which available water sources dry up and the affected area becomes dry and barren.

duff—The uppermost layer of decomposing vegetation that makes up the surface of a forest or jungle floor.

evaporation—The process in which liquid water is changed into a gaseous form and returned to the atmosphere.

halophytes—Crops that can be grown in water with a high salt content. Halophytes can be grown in areas near bodies of salt water where it is too expensive to remove the salt from the water.

hydroelectrical power generation—A type of power supply in which falling water is used to drive turbine engines.

hydrogeologists—Scientists who study water resources and the way they are used.

hydrological cycle—The cyclical process by which liquid water is used, returned to the atmosphere as gas, and then returned to the earth again in the form of precipitation.

instream usage—A type of water consumption in which water is used directly at the source.

irrigation—The process of bringing water in from a main source to use in watering crops.

leaching—The process whereby salts found in groundwater are deposited on the surface as the water evaporates and leaves behind residue.

lipids—Fatty substances found in living organisms. Scientists are experimenting using lipids from algae in creating fuel.

migratory—A term used to describe animals or birds that travel from one area to another during different times of the year. It most often refers to birds that travel to warmer climates during the winter months.

nonpoint sources—Areas of activity that can indirectly contaminate water supplies by creating pollutants that are washed into water sources by rain runoff. These include city streets, storm drains, mines, and feedlots.

nonpotable—A term used to describe water that is not fit to drink because of impurities.

offstream usage—A type of water consumption in which water is channeled from a main source to the point of usage.

osmosis—The process by which water is passed through the circulatory system of a tree or plant.

point sources—Areas of activity that can directly contaminate water supplies by creating pollutants that are deposited in water sources. These include landfills, dumps, and sewage disposal areas.

potable—A term used to describe water that is fit for drinking.

prior appropriation—A term used when discussing water rights. According to this principle, whoever first uses a water resource for beneficial purposes has main rights to that water source. Other users may use the source, but only if their use does not interfere with the primary user's needs.

rain fed farming—Farming that is based on the natural rainfall cycle of an area. Crops are grown during season when rain is expected, reducing the need for irrigation or other artificial forms of growth.

reclamation—The process in which areas covered by water is drained and turned into usable land.

reverse osmosis process—The process of forcing seawater through artificial membranes in order to remove the salt and create fresh water.

riparian reasonable use—A term used when discussing water rights. It refers to the right of someone who owns land adjoining or containing a water resource to use that resource.

salinization—The process of adding salts to soil and making it unfit for growing plants. Salinization can occur when there is poor drainage in an area.

selenium—A natural element which, when ingested in large amounts, can be deadly to humans and animals.

strata—The various layers that make up the earth's covering.

subsidence—The process whereby the surface of the earth sinks into the ground when the underlying soil has been stripped away by mining activity.

sustainable yield—A term used when discussing water rights. It means that the amount of water withdrawn from a water resource cannot exceed the amount of water the source can produce, no matter who owns the rights to the resource.

thermal distillation—A process in which salt is removed from seawater by forcing the water through a series of heated chambers, forcing out the salt in solid form and leaving fresh water.

thermoelectrical power generation—A type of power supply in which steam is used as a source of energy and water is used to cool reactors used in the process.

transpiration—The process in which water that is not used up by a plant is excreted through pores in the plant's leaves and returned to the atmosphere.

tributary—A smaller river or stream that is a branch or an off-shoot of a larger body of water.

trihalomethanes—Also called THMs. These compounds are formed when chlorine combines with organic matter found in water. They have been found to be cancer causing.

unconfined aquifer—An underground reservoir formed when water soaks into the ground and forms pools below the surface of the earth.

water table—The depth below ground at which water can be found.

water transfers—Also called water marketing. This term refers to the buying and selling of water rights from one user to another.

INDEX

Olga Cossi is the author of several books for young readers. Her book *The Magic Box* was named to the New York Public Library's "Books for the Teen Age" list, and *Harp Seals* was named an outstanding children's science trade book by the Children's Book Council and the National Science Teachers Association.

She lives in Coronado, California.